SEX SEGREGATION AND INEQUALITY IN THE MODERN LABOUR MARKET

Jude Browne

First published in Great Britain in November 2006 by

The Policy Press
University of Bristol
Fourth Floor
Beacon House
Queen's Road
Bristol BS8 1QU
UK

Tel +44 (0)117 331 4054
Fax +44 (0)117 331 4093
e-mail tpp-info@bristol.ac.uk
www.policypress.org.uk

Jude Browne is the Nuffield Foundation Research Fellow at the Centre for Research in the Arts, Social Sciences and Humanities, an Executive Director of the Cambridge University Centre for Gender Studies and a Fellow in Social and Political Sciences at Downing College, University of Cambridge.

British Library Cataloguing in Publication Data
A catalogue record for this book is available from the British Library.

Library of Congress Cataloging-in-Publication Data
A catalog record for this book has been requested.

ISBN-10 978 1 86134 599 2 hardcover
ISBN-13 978 1 86134 599 8 hardcover

Cover design by Qube Design Associates, Bristol.
Printed and bound by CPI Group (UK) Ltd, Croydon, CR0 4YY

Dedicated to Elizabeth and Patrick Browne

Contents

List of figures and tables

Figures

Tables

Acknowledgements

I would like to thank the Nuffield Foundation for funding me whilst writing this book and the Economic and Social Research Council for providing funds during the original research period.

I am wholly indebted to Daniel Beer, Duncan Bell, Bob Blackburn, Alison Carter, Simon Deakin, Sarah Fine, Bob Hepple, Ze'ev Emmerich, Marc Stears and Umar Salam for helping me to develop my thinking and to craft the writing of this book at various stages.

Introduction

Within all established liberal democracies, there is universal recognition that formal political, civil and social rights should apply equally to men and women. Within the economically developed world the idea of equality of opportunity, irrespective of sex, carries common currency across all shades of ideological opinion and is widely celebrated as both socially desirable and pragmatically sound. Since the 1970s, sophisticated anti-discrimination laws have evolved to combat prejudice-driven injustices and a multitude of strategies employed to resolve obstacles to equal opportunity for both sexes. For example, 'gender' is now 'mainstreamed' into state analysis of public policies, into corporations' assessment of their private behaviour, and even into the programmes of development offered abroad.

So ingrained has this notion become that one need only scan the mission statements of any international organisation, western governmental department or corporation to find the objective of 'gender equality' as a core tenet of institutional conduct.

Yet despite this apparent record of commitment to opening up opportunities to women as well as to men, key differences clearly remain between outcomes for each of the sexes. One such example is the distribution of economic resources, most notably pay and occupational status, which remain starkly unequal. This book seeks to engage with this problem in both theoretical and empirical terms. Its key line of argument is that there is a lack of fit between predominant definitions and explanations of occupational sex segregation on the one hand, and contemporary empirical evidence on the other. The consequences of this disjuncture are that the understandings of sex inequality that underpin our legal and policy approaches are out of date and, in fact, often counterproductive.

Central to this analysis is an assessment of the efficacy of various causal theories of sex segregation in the context of original quantitative and qualitative research conducted within a large British organisation – the British Broadcasting Corporation (BBC). It will be argued that problems associated with occupational sex segregation are not, as is frequently thought, primarily the result of the persistence of consciously restrictive patriarchal objectives, nor psychological essentialist accounts of sex difference, nor of freely made rational choices or preferences. They are rather the product of a 'systemic dissonance' between a revolution in contemporary social demands and poorly designed policy and legal frameworks.

A great deal of confusion surrounds the concepts related to 'occupational segregation' as they are deployed in labour market analysis and associated policy design. One might fruitfully address this conceptual vagueness by first calling into question the use of the term 'gender', which frames our discussions of equality between men and women. While this might initially appear a pedantic point it is one that requires closer scrutiny.

A note on 'gender'

In thinking about the question of which people should be treated equally and in what relevant respect this study will refer to 'sex segregation' and 'sex equality' rather than 'gender segregation' and 'gender equality'. I suggest that to use 'gender' for the purposes of constructing particular social and political *goals*, such as equality and justice, is confusing.

Today the terms 'gender' and 'sex' are frequently deployed indiscriminately, or, to be more precise, 'gender' is increasingly being used to cover both terms. It is, then, worth re-establishing the difference between the two concepts as used in the postwar context. From the late 1960s, 'sex' has been deemed a category of analysis that relates to the identification of an individual by biological endowments and functions. 'Gender' is concerned with the ascription of social characteristics such as 'womanly', 'manly', 'feminine' and 'masculine', which can be seen as culturally variable and not necessarily associated with the sex of an individual. While this distinction is admittedly rough around the edges, its general acceptance over the past 35 years heralded a rare, albeit minimal, consensus across mainstream academia: that the concept of sex is insufficient for describing social identities. Previously, 'sex' invoked an analysis of men and women based on an a priori set of assumptions about how each sex behaves. In an attempt to overcome what was seen as a cultural bias, the term 'gender' was introduced as a way of classifying individuals socially rather than biologically.

Bearing this distinction in mind then, what would it really mean to pursue 'gender equality' or 'gender justice', or to eradicate the 'gendered pay gap' or 'gender segregation'? To offer 'equality of gender' would presumably be to equalise the conditions of those pertaining to differing cultural codifications; to eradicate the 'gendered pay gap' would be to eradicate income differences between people who identify with, or are identified by, varying degrees of femininity or masculinity. This would be neither possible nor particularly desirable in the pursuit of any practical notion of societal justice. 'Gender' is not the relevant respect in which individuals should be rendered equal. 'Gender' is a description of countless characteristics and behaviours that may or may not be determined by sex. Surely, our focus is better articulated as the eradication of *discrimination* based on a range of differences (sex, sexuality, gender characteristics and so on) rather than, in effect, to suggest the actual pursuit of the equalisation of socially constructed gender traits. This is not to deny the importance of 'gender' as an analytical category, nor should it be understood as a return to outdated crude modes of analysis; this corrective is only possible in the wake of the past 35 years of 'gender analysis'. The concept's merits are clear when we consider the prejudiced assumptions made about an individual's abilities and capabilities according to sex or sexuality. Indisputably, one can have culturally identified 'feminine' or 'masculine' traits, or differing sexual preferences irrespective of one's biology, and, in this sense, the concept of gender is vitally different from traditional views on what it means in behavioural terms to be of a particular sex. But still, 'gender equality' as a societal goal is a problematic term and given the ambiguity that surrounds it, I suggest that in prescribing policy designed to combat empirical problems such as the durable pay gap between men and women, we should abandon 'gender' as a way of labelling objectives of equality.

I hope to show throughout this research, that those who discriminate (personally or institutionally, wittingly or unwittingly) base their judgements on stereotypes of sex, and it is in this sense that I claim we should address the use of negative stereotypes rather than aim for 'gender equality'.

Occupational sex segregation

The most important thing to note is that segregation is *not* synonymous with inequality. Equating the two is a mistake repeatedly made throughout academic, legal and policy literature. In its simplest terms, occupational sex segregation has two components: horizontal occupational sex segregation (HOSS) and vertical occupational sex segregation (VOSS). Yet only the latter is associated with inequality so we cannot say that sex segregation is equal to inequality. Before going into the detail of each of these components, it is also important to note that even where VOSS occurs (inequality), we should not immediately equate it with injustice, which would be to conflate observation with evaluation. Unequal outcomes are not always the product of prejudice or malpractice. However, for the moment we will assume that where VOSS does occur, it is at least a site worthy of investigation.

Following the Cambridge approach to occupational sex segregation (see Blackburn et al, 2001), the various necessary concepts are defined as follows.

Concentration is concerned with the sex composition of a labour force as indicated by the percentage of men and women. Jobs may be usefully categorised according to sex by comparing the sex concentration of one occupation or set of occupations to the sex concentration of an entire labour force. For example, the sex concentration of the British labour force is currently 46% female and 54% male. Hence any occupation or group of occupations with a female concentration of 46% or over is classified as a 'female job'. Effectively the female (or male) concentration level of a given workforce becomes the 'cut-off' point for determining the 'sex' of its occupations. When analysing labour force data, it is often useful to re-group the data into three categories: 'female' occupations', 'male' occupations and 'mixed' occupations. Mixed occupations are those whose concentration is closely related to the male and female concentration of the total labour force and tend to be the highest paying occupations. In this study, I have used a 10% margin either side of the female concentration of the total case study labour force, which generates some very interesting comparisons between 'mixed' occupations and 'female' and 'male' occupations.

Occupational sex segregation is a property of a *total* given labour force. Occupational sex segregation is the *tendency* for men and women to be employed in different occupations from each other across all the occupations under analysis. It is an assessment as to how far the concentrations of men and women in different occupations deviate from the 'unsegregated' labour force in which every occupation reflects the sex ratios of the workforce as a whole. As occupational sex segregation has two components, HOSS and VOSS, we refer to it as *overall* occupational sex segregation to avoid more confusion.

VOSS is the *inequality* dimension of overall segregation. Whereas the consideration of whether a workforce displays overall segregation depends on nothing more than the concentration of all occupations by sex, determining if there is inequality requires the introduction of some ordinal scale. Within the setting of a labour force, the most obvious value that we can attribute to 'inequality' is pay. VOSS then, refers to the disproportionate distribution of men and women across occupations, which, when on a hierarchical (vertical) scale indicative of pay levels, will reveal quantitative inequalities between the sexes in employment. It is a statistical measurement of the correlation between the orderings of occupations by sex and by pay.

HOSS is a dimension that simply indicates *difference* (in occupational terms) that does not comprise pay inequalities. For example, if all women and men were completely segregated into different occupations (total segregation) but everyone was paid the same then there would be no 'inequality', only difference. Consequently, there would be no correlation between sex and pay and the vertical dimension (VOSS) would be zero with overall segregation being comprised entirely of the horizontal dimension (HOSS).

In reality, however, segregation tends to possess a messy combination of both horizontal and vertical dimensions, as even when there is a degree of inequality, its correlation with sex is far from absolute. The measurement of these dimensional quantities provides, therefore, a method by which the level of segregation corresponding to inequality can be determined. Moreover, as quantitative data, it allows a comparison of one workforce with another. The relationship of the two dimensions to each other is somewhat complex but one example to consider would be two occupations within a workplace, one with a high concentration of women and the other with a high concentration of men, where the male job is remunerated at a rate far below that of the female job. The high concentrations within the occupations result in a contribution to the figure for overall segregation but the reverse bias (against the correlation of male jobs with high pay) will diminish the value for VOSS. Thus, a workplace in which we find some well-paid female jobs, or badly paid male jobs, will display a level of segregation composed more of the horizontal than the vertical dimension. The way in which overall, horizontal and vertical dimensions relate will be discussed in more detail when the method of calculating a numerical value for VOSS is set out in the quantitative analysis of the BBC case study.

Misinterpretation of concepts: what follows are some examples of how the concepts of segregation are commonly misconstrued:

> ### Example 1:
>
> Segregation has taken various forms; either an occupation has been predominantly male or female (vertical segregation) or women have congregated in the lowest grades of mixed jobs (horizontal segregation). (Fredman, 1997, p 103)

Fredman's first definition (of vertical segregation) is in fact describing the *concentration* of men and women into different occupations without any special reference to pay inequalities. In her second definition (horizontal segregation), the disparity of pay between men and women is actually a description of VOSS; furthermore, this pay disparity is not exclusive to 'mixed jobs' but to all occupations within a labour force.

> ### Example 2:
>
> ...'clerks' and 'managers' are classified as different occupations, but 'clerks' are also subordinate to 'managers'. Does the fact that women are a majority of those in clerical occupations reflect horizontal or vertical segregation? In practice, an answer to this question would have to take into account whether or not clerical jobs were linked to managerial jobs in a promotion hierarchy. (Crompton, 1997, p 44)

Again, this example is in fact referring to the *concentration* of men and women into two occupations rather than occupational sex segregation across a labour force. The question is not whether these two jobs are linked by a promotional hierarchy per se, but rather how much each job, in terms of its sex concentration and pay level, contributes to the horizontal and vertical dimensions of overall segregation. In this example, because 'clerks' tend to be much lower paid than 'managers', and 'clerk' is a female-dominated occupation and 'manager' is a male-dominated occupation, their contribution to overall segregation would be high levels of *both* HOSS and VOSS.

> ### Example 3:
>
> Horizontal segregation is where the workforce of a particular industry or sector is mostly made up of one particular gender. An example of horizontal segregation can be found in construction where men make up 90% of the industry's workforce, whereas childcare is almost exclusively a female occupation. Vertical segregation is where opportunities for career

progression within an industry or sector for a particular gender are narrowed. Vertical segregation disproportionately affects women more than men. For example, women are less likely to work as managers or senior officials than men – just 11% of all women in employment compared to 18% of men. (Women and Equality Unit, 2006, p1)

With this example, it is assumed that VOSS is a strategy rather than a quantitative measurement, while HOSS is understood to be associated strictly within industries and sectors – that is, concentration. Neither is correct.

Example 4:

... we now know that there is no direct link between occupational segregation and the pay gap; the association is coincidental rather than causal, and the two processes are independently socially constructed. (Hakim, forthcoming: 2007)

As we have seen there may well be a direct link between (overall) segregation and the pay gap: it is precisely this correlation that is measured by vertical segregation.

These are but a few examples that illustrate the importance of concept clarification within the field of occupational sex segregation.

The British context

The contemporary British labour market will be used as the general context in which VOSS is explored. As a liberal democratic state with well-established and sophisticated civil, political and social rights it provides a good case study setting in which to analyse VOSS (see Appendix 1 for examples of legislation that has promoted equality between the sexes in Britain). The following collection of data pertaining to the contemporary British labour market indicates both similarities and differences in the economic and social situations of men and women and can be used to contextualise the explanatory theories of VOSS and case study material throughout the book.

Population: currently Britain's population stands at 59.2 million, 30.3 million of whom are women and 28.9 million men (Office for National Statistics [ONS]: Census, April 2001). From the age of 22, females outnumber males through all age groups. The most marked difference in numbers occurs in the over-50s age group in which women enjoy greater life expectancy. The average life expectancy (at birth) of females is 80 years compared to only 76 for males. Consequently, there are approximately three times as many widows as widowers (ONS: Census, April 2001).

Habitation arrangements: six out of every 10 men and women live in a couple (5 in 10 married and 1 in 10 cohabiting). The majority of these couples living together are both employed: 63% are dual-earning households (ONS: Census, April 2001; Quarterly Labour Force [QLF] Survey, December 2004-February 2005; Household and Family Data, 2001). However, there has also been a sharp rise in the number of single-parent households that now stand at 6% of the total, a figure that has doubled since the 1970s (ONS: Labour Force Survey [LFS], Spring 2002). Half of lone mothers with dependent children live in social sector housing indicating low income.

Marriage and divorce: the average age at marriage has increased by seven years since 1971. Today the average man marries at the age of 35 years and the average woman at the age of 32 years (this includes subsequent marriages to the first). There has been a sharp rise in divorce, which stood at 1.5 million divorced men and 2.0 million divorced women in 2001, compared with 187,000 and 296,000 divorced men and women, respectively, in 1971 (ONS: Census, April 2001).

Education: girls outperform boys at GCSE and 'A' level. In 2002 58% of girls achieved five or more GCSE grades at A*-C compared with only 47% of boys. At 'A' level, 43% of females gained two or more compared to only 34% of males. With the exception of General Studies and English Literature, females outperformed males in all subjects at 'A' level, including mathematics. For those at undergraduate level, males and females are as likely as each other to obtain a first class degree (DfES, 2002).

There has been a vast increase in the number of female undergraduates over recent decades. For example, in 1966 only 28% of undergraduates were female, in 1981 this percentage rose to 39%, 44% in 1987 to a current majority of 54%. However, subjects at degree level tend to be relatively segregated according to sex: Education (81% female, 19% male); Languages (72% female, 28% male); Biological sciences (64% female, 36% male); Law (62% female, 36% male); Physical sciences (40% female, 60% male); Computer science (20% female, 80% male); Engineering and technology (15% female, 85% male).

Only Medicine, History, Philosophy and Business-related subjects tend to be sex neutral (EOC, 2005).

Employment: the British labour force is almost half female, at 46%. Of those women, 56% work full time compared to 89% of men. Despite the large increase in women's employment, they are far more likely to work part time, at 44%, compared to 11% of economically active men.

The nature of work has changed extensively since the 1980s when one in three male employees was working in manufacturing industries. This proportion has now fallen to one in five, partly as a consequence of the de-industrialisation of Britain that has been taking place over the past three decades. Consequently, and in alignment with developments in new technologies, there has been a considerable decrease in manual labour. In contrast there has been sizeable growth in the service sector of the British labour market, which has opened up significant employment opportunities for women. In the mid-1980s men filled 2.5 million more jobs than women; 20 years later men and women are almost equally represented – with 13 million jobs occupied by men and 12.8 million by women – although nearly half of the latter are working part time (ONS: LFS, Spring 2003; Labour Market Trends, November 2003).

Figure A: Percentage of people in occupational group by sex

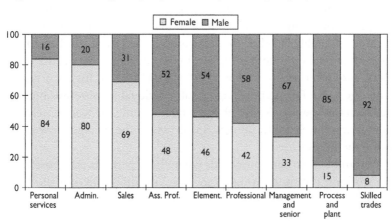

Key: 1: Personal services; 2: Administrative and secretarial; 3: Sales and customer services; 4: Associate professional and technical; 5: Elementary; 6: Professional; 7: Managers and senior officials; 8: Process, plant and machine operatives; 9: Skilled trades.

Source: ONS *Labour Force Survey*, Spring 2004

Despite these transformations, however, women and men tend to be employed in different occupations. Indicative of overall occupational sex segregation, most women are employed in occupations where women predominate. Using broad categories of occupations as shown in Figure A, these groups were 'Personal services', 'Administrative and secretarial', 'Sales and customer services' occupations.

Figure A is indicative of substantial overall occupational sex segregation within the labour market, that is, of the tendency for women and men to be segregated across different occupations. In terms of basic analysis, these data can be split into 'female', 'male' and 'mixed' occupational categories. Given that the female concentration of Britain's labour market is 46%, the occupational categories of 'Personal services', 'Administrative and secretarial', 'Sales and customer services' can be termed as 'female' occupational categories; 'Associate professional and technical' and 'Elementary' and 'Professional' are 'mixed'; and finally 'Managers and senior officials', 'Process, plant and machine operatives' and 'Skilled trades' can be termed as 'male'.

Pay: since the 1970 Equal Pay Act took effect (and also the introduction of paid maternity leave) in 1975, there has been a clear increase in women's pay. In 1970 women working full time were only earning 54% of average weekly earnings of men. This figure now stands at 82% and has been relatively stable for the past decade. For part-time working women, the pay gap stands at a staggering 40%.

The average weekly individual income for men is £408 compared to £227 for women (DTI, 2005). Individual incomes for women were considerably less than those for men across all age bands. Average total individual income was highest for women aged between 25 and 29 at £249 per week. This was 76% of the average for men in the same age band. For men, average total individual income was highest between the ages of 35 and 49. Individual income for women relative to men was lowest for those aged 55-59, where the average for women was only 42% of men's.

Within dual-earner households where both partners (heterosexual) are working full time, women's income constitutes 45% of the total household income and men's, 55% (DTI, 2005). This, unsurprisingly, contrasts sharply with households where women work part time or do not work because of parenting duties. In these cases, women who work part time contribute only 27% of total family income and for those who do not work only 9% (much of which is generated by state benefit) (DTI, 2005). Men with children tend to earn more than other groups partly because they tend to work the longest hours. Lone

Figure B: Pay gap between full-time working men and women by occupational group

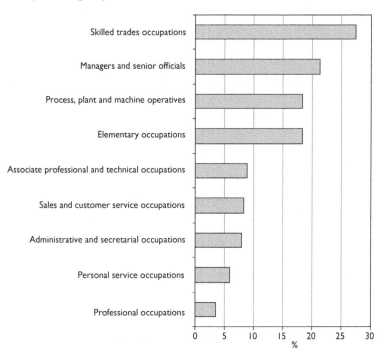

Source: ONS Annual Survey of Hours and Earnings, 2005

mothers are in receipt of the highest level of benefits in the British working-age population, receiving 37% of their total weekly income from benefits, inferring low levels of earnings. Female pensioners are far more likely to be dependent on state benefits than income from occupational or personal pensions than their male counterparts.

Figure B illustrates the pay gap between men and women in each of these occupational groups. As we can see the largest gaps are within male-dominated occupational groups: 'Skilled trades' (27.5%); 'Managers and senior officials' (21.4%); and 'Process, plant and machine operatives' (18.3%). These sectors tend to command better pay than the female-dominated occupational groups (where there is also less of a pay gap). However, the smallest pay gap of all is in the highest paid occupational category, the professional occupations, where the pay gap is just 3.5%.

These kinds of trends that illustrate how sex concentration relates to pay will be analysed in greater detail within the case study analysis in subsequent chapters.

Working parents: of mothers with children of under 5 years, 55% are in employment compared to 73% of those with children between the ages of 5 and 10. This latter figure is a comparable number to non-mothers of working age, 76% of whom are employed. However, 40% of women with dependent children work part time. Only 4% of men with dependent children work part time compared to those who work full time at 93% (regardless of the age of their children). Lone mothers are far less likely to work (only 56% are in employment) compared to cohabiting or married mothers (at 72%). Moreover, lone mothers are far more likely to be economically active if their child is over 5 years of age. Only 38% of lone mothers with children younger than 5 compared to 60% with older children were economically active in 2003. Particularly noteworthy is the fact that the difference in economic activity rates between lone mothers and cohabiting or married mothers evaporates as children reach adulthood (at 16-18 years) (ONS: LFS, Spring 2003).

Methodological pointers

This study has investigated VOSS in an employment environment, which has not only complied fully with British and European legislation and best practice guides to sex equality, but has also made a concerted effort to provide an equal playing field on which men and women could compete for the jobs they wish to occupy and more generally where women do not suffer obvious discrimination or bias. The rationale for choosing such a setting was twofold. First, it provided a control for, as much as possible, the obvious negative effects of malpractice or institutional inertia thereby permitting an assessment of efficacy of current policy approaches. Second, it provided a kind of laboratory in which to test the various claims of prominent causal theories of VOSS. Accordingly, a large workforce of both male and female full-time workers, employed on continuing long-term contracts in an attractive and competitive employment setting, framed by progressive equality policies, was identified as a case study. Part-time workers and short-term contract workers were not included in the analysis as the aim was to examine the causes of VOSS between male and female workers who enjoyed comparable career opportunities, employment security and prospective pay scales[1].

The BBC as a case study

The BBC, established in 1922, is a publicly owned organisation dedicated to public service broadcasting. Its status is governed by a Royal Charter and Agreement that is periodically renegotiated with the current government. The BBC is regulated by a board of 12 governors who act as trustees of the public interest and is mainly funded by a licence fee that is levied as a flat-rate tax on all households using a television[2]. It is the largest and oldest broadcasting corporation in Britain, serving 450 million homes worldwide. This research should not be understood as a study of the BBC per se but rather of a workforce that enjoys a particular set of working conditions[3]. As a case study in which to analyse VOSS, the BBC held two main attractions:

- the BBC is renowned for its progressive sex equality policies and ethos;
- the BBC is a highly competitive and attractive employment environment for large numbers of both male and female full-time workers.

A recent BBC Governor's objective report states: "Gender representation is a real success story. Around 50% of staff and 37% of senior management are women"[4]. Similarly, the Kingsmill Review of Women's Employment and Pay (commissioned by the British Cabinet Office) refers to the BBC as a 'pioneer' in terms of its equality strategies (Kingsmill, 2001, p 51). These successes may in part be due to the BBC's status as a publicly owned corporation. As the foreword to the BBC's Managers' Guidelines states, "As a public service organisation the BBC must be able to stand the test of public and parliamentary scrutiny" (p 1). Several researchers have noted that public organisations tend to provide better working and promotion opportunities for women, as they are motivated by governmental monitoring (see, for example, Prandy et al, 1983; Burchell and Rubery, 1990; Crompton and Sanderson, 1990; Burchell, 1996). Accordingly, in addition to seeking to meet its basic statutory obligations with regard to anti-discrimination law, the BBC developed extensive internal guidelines on sex equality policy. It adopted codes of practice devised by the Equal Opportunities Commission (EOC), employed external specialists to conduct analysis of the internal mechanisms of its recruitment and training practices and offered specific career training to female employees. It produced several internal publications focused on the issue of employee equality, conducted in-house surveys on working conditions of all its employees (using anonymous questionnaires), and infused all of its managerial objectives with annual 'gender targets'. Primarily managers are responsible for equal opportunities. However, each BBC subsection (directorate) has a chief personnel officer who, together with a specialist equal opportunities officer, is responsible for overseeing that equal opportunities issues are fully implemented in all aspects of the directorate's procedures. Each manager is instructed to ensure that principles of equality are integrated into the everyday working practice of their department or section.

As a result, the BBC prides itself as a "pioneer in introducing flexible and progressive arrangements and benefits for staff" (BBC Annual Report, 1997/98, p 35).

Based on this equal opportunities ethos, the BBC offers extensive in-house employee benefits, in excess of statutory provision. These include: maternity benefits, paternity leave, adoption leave, family leave, childcare support, flexible working arrangements, and a career break scheme:

> The BBC recognises that most people have caring responsibilities at some time in their working lives and is committed to helping staff reconcile work and personal responsibilities. Helping staff to meet these obligations is a key part of the BBC's policy on equality of opportunity.... Within the BBC, it is recognised that caring responsibilities are not restricted to childcare, a growing number of employees provide care for older or disabled dependants. Men can share the same problems of reconciling work and family life as women, and problems can be exacerbated by attitudes based upon stereotypes. To help meet the BBC's gender targets we must operate flexible employment policies. (BBC Managers' Guidelines, People in Focus, Section B, p 1; unpublished)

At the time of data collection at the end of 1990s, the BBC full-time workforce was 19,129, the sex concentration of which was 49% female and 51% male working within 79 different types of occupation. Moreover, the BBC's policy was to employ the majority of staff for the longest duration possible, as this is deemed to be advantageous in producing the following:

> ... commitment between manager and staff member;
> continuity, both in terms of support to the business unit

and clarity in the individual's employment status; straightforward administration; flexibility in deployment; and more predictable costs. (BBC's Manager's Guidelines, People in Focus, Section C1, Contract, p 2 of Section 14; unpublished)

The BBC's Manager's Guidelines clearly instruct that:

> ... constant renewal of fixed-term contracts over a period of years should be avoided. Unless there are overriding managerial reasons why the fixed term arrangement should continue ... positive consideration should be given to transferring staff to continuing contracts. (BBC's Management Guidelines, People in Focus, Section C1, Contract, p 9 of Section 14; unpublished)

The BBC's preference for employing staff on continuing contracts is a positive aspect for many staff. During the period of data collection, 75% of the BBC's full-time workforce was employed on continuing long-term contracts.

That the BBC is held in very high public esteem contributes to its popularity as an employer attracting highly competitive and skilled applicants. In this way, the BBC offers a particularly interesting environment in which to analyse the occupational status of men and women who firstly, work in an attractive employment environment and secondly, are deemed to be of a generally high calibre. All staff under analysis were working full time, employed on a full long-term contract and subject to the same regulations, benefits and pay scales.

Structure of the book

Chapter One provides a critical analysis of causal explanations of VOSS. Those under scrutiny span both standard and developed versions of three broadly defined perspectives on why sex segregation occurs and persists. Theoretical approaches, which proceed from a binary understanding of male and female psychological and/or physiological attributes include Steven Goldberg's Male Dominance Theory, Simon Baron-Cohen's new Empathising/Systemising Theory and also Carol Gilligan's Different Voice' thesis. The work of Sylvia Walby and Valerie Bryson assigns primary causality of VOSS to forms of patriarchy and the oppressive practices that serve to sustain it. Finally, Gary Becker's Rational Choice Theory and Catherine Hakim's Preference Theory seek to account for VOSS in terms of the distribution and deployment of human capital. Chapter Two provides an in-depth quantitative account of sex segregation within the BBC's full-time workforce, which, despite commendable institutional efforts, has remained considerable. Within this chapter there is a fuller description of how the two constitutive components of overall occupational sex segregation, the vertical and horizontal dimensions, relate to each other. Chapter Three sets out a detailed qualitative study of BBC staff views on sex segregation within their place of work and offers a number of illuminating insights into why VOSS persists. Chapter Four is a critical assessment of current legal and policy approaches to sex inequality in Britain and provides a specific focus on the Equal Treatment Principle (ETP), which underpins all European Union (EU) member equality and anti-sex discrimination law. It also considers the legal and policy implications of the various causal theories under investigation throughout the book. Finally, the concluding chapter summarises the main arguments of this research and suggests future policy directions.

Notes

[1] As we saw earlier, the vast majority of part-time workers are female (89%), tend to occupy lower-status occupations and earn 40% less than their male counterparts. Part-time work and women's disproportionate low pay have been the subject of numerous studies and the correlation between the two has been well established (see, for example, Rubery et al, 1994; Fagan and O'Reilly, 1998; Joshi and Paci, 1998).

[2] Although it also receives grants for free television licenses issued to people aged 75 or over, as well as revenues from its commercial activities, linked to BBC Worldwide and BBC Ventures Group.

[3] The BBC is an extremely complex institution that has undergone extensive organisational change. During the past decade, for example, it converted some of its departments into an entity of limited company status that became a wholly owned subsidiary of the BBC. These changes fall beyond the remit of this book and are not analysed.

[4] See www.bbcgovernors.co.uk/docs/objectives04.html

ONE

Explanations of occupational sex segregation

How effective are prominent causal theories of VOSS? This chapter assesses representative theories from three major 'explanatory camps': psychological and psycho-physiological theories, theories of patriarchy, and human capital-based theories. The claims of these approaches will be tested against the findings of an in-depth case study of BBC workers over subsequent chapters.

The following sections examine the work both of more 'traditional' advocates of each camp and of some theorists who have attempted to develop their fields. The intention is to provide a broader account of the various approaches and to emphasise the problematic features of each perspective, pointing towards the need for a more convincing and holistic explanation of VOSS.

Psychological and psycho-physiological theories: 'binary-based' accounts

Some experimental psychologists such as Simon Baron-Cohen have recently returned what might be called the 'the biology of gender' thesis to the forefront of the sex/gender debate. New scientifically based research combining physiological, psychological and behavioural testing are interpreted as showing that 'gendered behaviour' is essentially biologically driven. Such arguments are rapidly gaining currency across the social sciences and are often to be found at the root of many economic approaches to sex inequality, such as human capital-based theories (see Dupré, 2001). Here we shall look at two examples of the 'biology of gender' approach: Steven Goldberg's Male Dominance Theory and the more recent work of Simon Baron-Cohen's Empathising/Systemising Theory. Although Baron-Cohen is keen not to be seen as a 'reductionist' (a label often given to Goldberg), the following account illustrates quite striking similarities between their respective theories.

Also included in what I have termed collectively the 'binary-based' accounts of sex inequality is Carol Gilligan's Different Voice thesis. Gilligan is not explicit about the causal nature of distinct differences between men's and women's behaviour, and in this sense she certainly cannot be classified as a biological essentialist. Her arguments, nevertheless, chime with those of Baron-Cohen and it is for this reason that I have incorporated her work here.

Goldberg and Male Dominance Theory

Steven Goldberg's elaborate thesis (1979, 1993) essentially states that 'male supremacy' is 'inevitable' in any given hierarchy. VOSS is therefore easily explicable within the context of a modern labour market stratified by status and pay levels. Men and women, he argues, are predisposed to assume dichotomous unequal social positions due to their physiological and psychological differences.

Goldberg draws on a wide range of psycho-pharmacological research on differences in average animal and human performance, examining such questions as whether males or females are faster, stronger, and so on. He combines the results of these experiments with the results of physiological tests that measure the differences in average blood concentrations of hormones in females and males. In short, the basis of the Male Dominance Theory is that certain hormones (testosterone in particular) equip men with an 'aggressive advantage' over women. In behavioural terms, this advantage translates into social differences between men and women. This, Goldberg maintains, explains why all supra-familial levels of organisation are 'patriarchal', by which he means "any system or organisation (political, economic, industrial, financial, religious, or social) in which the overwhelming number of upper positions in hierarchies, are occupied by males" (Goldberg, 1979, p 29). Aided by the hormonally driven 'aggressive advantage', men are far more likely to be competitive, self-assertive, and dominant in their approach to hierarchical contexts such as the labour market; as he contends, "in every society males attain the high status (non-maternal) roles and positions and perform the high status tasks, whatever those tasks are" (Goldberg, 1979, p 50).

Goldberg does not deny that social factors affect behaviour, but he argues that these serve to enhance the effects of differing hormonal endowments of men and women. "Socialisation", he maintains, conforms to behavioural patterns determined by neuro-endocrinological differences between the sexes and is highly "efficient", since it enables societal institutions effectively to utilise the natural disparities between men and women, as for example, reflected in VOSS (Goldberg, 1993, p 105). Hegemonic social expectations for 'male dominance', most obvious in sexual relationships, emerge in all settings, including the workplace, and the consequent pattern of inequality that materialises between men and women is explained as a "manifestation of the psycho-physiological reality" (Goldberg, 1979, p 29):

> ... a *feeling* acknowledged by the emotions of both men and women that general authority in dyadic and familial relationships, in whatever terms a particular society defines authority, ultimately resides in the male. (Goldberg, 1979, p 41)

Goldberg does not claim that males are necessarily more capable than females of performing tasks at higher occupational levels. Rather, he maintains that men are more likely to pursue high-status positions in the first place. While he does mention cases of 'exceptional' women, citing the example of former British Prime Minister, Margaret Thatcher, he emphasises that women who have achieved high employment status are *exceptional* and do not tell us anything about the comparison of average men and women. Thus, in Goldberg's view, high-status occupations are male dominated not because women lack the ability to perform the necessary duties of the job, but because any role that bestows high status will attract more male candidates than female candidates (Goldberg, 1993, p 108). The essence of this argument is that males are more likely and more willing to compete than women in any given competitive setting.

Goldberg claims that men and women would be socially equal if we were to remove hierarchies from social environments, that is, if we were to remove the competitive element of social life. However, he goes on to clarify:

> Since there are no societies totally lacking in hierarchy, and since there is clear male dominance in the few that have little formal hierarchy, we can ignore the theoretical possibility of a society without hierarchy. (Goldberg, 1993, p 16)

Male Dominance Theory is based on a reductionist biological account of differences between males and females. However, it appears that its logic may serve many other approaches to social inequality between men and women. For example, Catherine Hakim, writer of the human capital-based Preference Theory, states that "on the evidence, Goldberg's theory of male dominance and patriarchy is unassailable" (1996, p 212). This is a view to which we shall return later.

Despite the appeal of Male Dominance Theory to some, it suffers from several fundamental weaknesses, both empirical and theoretical. Most important of these is the over-simplistic relationship drawn between testosterone-induced aggression and social advantage. The impact of external social structures and institutions is largely ignored or undervalued in Goldberg's account and consequently he does not reflect on possible solutions to sex inequality. Indeed, it would appear that policy approaches to minimise social sex inequality are futile or counterproductive, given the existence of efficient, biologically driven divisions of labour between men and women, who are equipped with differing abilities.

Goldberg's simplistic inferences can be met with equally straightforward challenges. For example, although men generally produce higher testosterone levels than women, higher levels of testosterone do not necessarily result in aggressive behaviour. As critics of biological determinist theories have pointed out, social environment is far more likely to be a determinant of human action and behaviour (see, for example, Lowe and Hubbard, 1983; Connell, 1987). Hence, to make assumptions about the general aggression levels and particular behavioural traits of men is unjustified. Goldstein, after surveying a wide range of interdisciplinary literatures on the impact of testosterone levels on social behaviour, concludes:

> The evidence on the entire question of testosterone and aggression in humans is undermined by problems of measurement, reverse causality, and poor experimental design. The main conclusion is that testosterone seems to influence intensity of aggression in some contexts, that these are not well understood and are not dramatic in magnitude. (Goldstein, 2001, p 153)

The claim that behavioural differences between men and women are explained simply by sex differences is further weakened by the fact that homosexuals do not tend to fit into stereotypical 'traditional' sex roles or behavioural patterns. Although some homosexual men are seen as having more feminine 'traits' than masculine ones, there is no evidence to suggest that they are generally less competitive in personality or have lower testosterone levels than heterosexual men (Goldstein, 2001). To follow Goldberg's argument, one might assume that this would be the case. Furthermore, as Pilcher (1999, p 2) points out, "adult transsexuals ... challenge the dichotomy between 'naturally' male and 'naturally' female bodies [and] more generally, people routinely transform their 'natural' bodies in order to make them become more or less, 'male' or 'female'"[1]. The issue of sexual orientation is not discussed in this book, but these facts are obvious limitations on a reductionist biological approach to the social behaviour of men and women (see Treadwell, 1987; Butler, 1990; Carver, forthcoming: 2007).

A further consideration in assessing Male Dominance Theory is the sizeable improvement in women's educational attainment. As illustrated in the introduction, now women outperform men even in traditionally 'male' subjects, and yet there is no suggestion that women's testosterone levels are increasing, or that hierarchies are diminishing. The same is certainly true of the professional occupations, in which men and women are represented relatively equally in the highest paid sector of the labour market (this is a trend to which we will return in the empirical study of the BBC in later chapters).

Goldberg's theory can further be challenged on methodological grounds. Sayers (1982), for example, criticises the construction of ethnocentric and androcentric conceptions of human behaviour from experiments on animals. Similarly Bleier (1984) and Rose (1987) assert that the observation of animal behaviour tells us nothing about the workings of *human social institutions*. Even in the direct comparison of humans, to move from *average* differences in hormone levels to *categorical* differences in social behaviour is an unpersuasive approach (Connell, 1987).

Goldberg is of the view that the mere existence of hierarchies 'ignites' the mechanisms of male attainment and consequently male dominance, a view endorsed by Hakim:

> Men never need to be encouraged to apply for promotion, whereas women do. The example is often quoted of the job advertisement that failed to attract any women applicants at all until the salary was reduced by half in a re-advertisement. (Hakim, 1996, p 8; 1979, p 50)

However, could it not easily be the case that many women expect to be employed in lower-level jobs and paid at a lower rate? Certainly, the empirical evidence set out in the Introduction suggests that this is what they should expect. An observation of women's lower average employment status, however, says nothing about women's preferences, or whether or not they are deserving of higher earnings. Any lack of female competition in such situations is likely to be a case of societal limitations and low expectations rather than an innate lack of competitiveness. In her extensive writings on this subject, Nussbaum has claimed that people can adapt to certain adverse circumstances and unwittingly fail to mobilise themselves to effect change. This she calls 'adaptive preferences' (see Nussbaum, 2000).

Furthermore, Goldberg assumes that there is an environment of open competition between men and women within the labour market, whereby individuals are free to compete along the lines of a simple meritocracy. However, there is not, and has never has been, an equal playing field free of social prejudices, in which men and women can compete according to their personal capabilities.

While the sexes are clearly biologically different, it seems implausible to assume that women are, as a group of diverse heterogeneous individuals, inherently less determined or competitive than men per se, particularly in terms of employment institutions. We simply cannot ignore the psychological and anthropological research that has overwhelmingly concluded that social factors are the major constructors of identity and behaviour (Oakley, 1972; Friedl, 1975; Erhardt and Meyer-Bahlburg, 1981; Pilcher, 1999; see Spelke in Pinker and Spelke, 2005). As Connell states, "sociobiology for all its claims to scientific explanation cannot produce for inspection the mechanisms of biological causation ... [and] is reduced to speculations" (Connell, 1987, p 69).

Finally, we return to Goldberg's primary device, the male 'aggressive advantage', which he uses to explain men's superior positioning across the labour market. Are we to assume that half the population (male) knows how to harness apparent biological aggressiveness into effective levels of determination or confidence in order to secure top jobs? Surely these qualities are far more likely to be complex personality traits, constructed by diverse personal experience, rather than a supposed universal male biological predisposition to psycho-physical aggression? Goldberg asserts that men's aptitude for 'competitiveness' is superior to that of women. However, if we consider for example, sample A, comprising two female violinists competing vigorously in a musical competition and sample B, comprising two males competing vigorously in a game of drafts, we would be unable to assess which sex is more capable of 'competitiveness'. Goldberg's point, to recall, is that men are more *competitive*, not that they are innately superior when it comes to particular tasks. But what would it matter if Milo were more competitive than Millie, if Millie were the better violinist? It would appear that Goldberg's only justification (an untenable one) for claiming that men are more able to compete for higher status positions due to their 'aggressive advantage' is that they are generally over-represented in the high end of hierarchies. This, however, is merely a retrospective assumption based on the status quo. It tells us nothing about *why* such differences occur.

Baron-Cohen and Empathising/Systemising Theory

Simon Baron-Cohen, a leading figure in the field of experimental psychology, has recently presented the Empathising/Systemising Theory. Baron-Cohen proposes that "the female brain is predominantly hard-wired for empathy" and that "the male brain is predominantly hard-wired for understanding and building systems" (Baron-Cohen, 2003, p 1). 'Empathising' describes the ability to classify another person's emotions and to respond to them appropriately (brain type E). This means to make sense of the behaviour of others and to form a degree of attachment to their feelings and experiences. 'Systemising' refers to the exploration of systems and their laws, rules and mechanisms (brain type S); this demands emotional detachment from others so as to facilitate the selection of relevant information and the ability to make impartial assessments. Baron-Cohen describes these two systems as "wholly different kinds of processes" which are "not mystical ... but grounded in our neurophysiology" (Baron-Cohen, 2003, pp 5-6).

Like Goldberg, Baron-Cohen argues that there is a more competitive streak in males; however, he focuses on the differing cerebral abilities of men and women. He remains adamant that his is not a crude reductionist account of why men and women are treated differently socially (as in the case of VOSS). He takes great care to explain that his theory explores averages of sex difference, and that these should not be confused with stereotypes like those implied by Male Dominance Theory, for example. Stereotypes, he maintains, are based on a set of assumptions about a group and serve to reduce the individual to the average. Baron-Cohen insists that each individual should be treated as just that, an individual. Accordingly, he argues that anyone could have the brain type S (systemising) or the brain type E (empathising) or, indeed, the brain type B (balanced between the two). However, crucially, he does argue that there *are* essential differences between the two most frequently found types of brain, that is, the E type most commonly found in women and the S type most commonly found in men.

Baron-Cohen's sources are extensive and he draws on numerous scientific experiments on male and female behaviour. The following are examples of Baron-Cohen's summaries of results that illustrate his approach. (All of the following examples and references are cited in Baron-Cohen, 2003.)

- *Sharing and turn taking:* on average, girls show more concern for fairness, while boys tend to share resources less than girls. In one study, boys were 50 times more competitive than girls, while girls were 20 times more likely than boys to take turns in group activities (Charlesworth and Dzur, 1987).
- *Values in relationships:* more women than men value the development of altruistic, reciprocal relationships that, by definition, require empathy. In contrast, more men value power, politics and competition (Ahlgren and Johnson, 1979). Girls are more likely to endorse cooperative items on a questionnaire and to rate the establishment of intimacy as more important than the establishment of dominance. In contrast, boys are more likely than girls to endorse competitive items and to rate social status as more important than intimacy (Knight and Chao, 1989).
- *Aggression:* even in average quantities, aggression only occurs with reduced levels of empathy. Males tend to show far more 'direct' aggression (pushing, hitting, punching and so on), while females tend to show more 'indirect' (relational, covert) aggression (including gossip, exclusion and cutting remarks). Direct aggression may require an even lower level of empathy than indirect aggression (Crick and Grotpeter, 1995).
- *Establishing a 'dominance hierarchy':* males are quicker to establish hierarchies. This, in part, reflects their lower 'empathising skills', because often a hierarchy is established by one person pushing others around in order to become the leader (Strayer, 1980).
- *Language style:* girls' speech is more cooperative, reciprocal and collaborative. In concrete terms, this is also reflected in girls being able to continue a conversational exchange with a partner for a longer period. When girls disagree, they are more likely to express their difference of opinion sensitively, in the form of a question rather than an assertion. Boys' way of communicating verbally involves more 'single-voiced discourse', where the speaker presents only his own perspective. The female speech style exhibits more 'double-voiced discourse'; girls spend more time negotiating with their partners, trying to take the other person's wishes into account (Smith, 1985).
- *Parenting style:* fathers are less likely than mothers to hold their infants in a face-to-face position. Mothers are more likely to follow through the child's choice of topic in play, while fathers are more

likely to impose their own topic. Also, mothers fine-tune their speech more often to match their children's understanding (Power, 1985).

- *Toy preferences:* boys are more interested than girls in toy vehicles, weapons, building blocks and mechanical toys, all of which are open to being 'systemised' (Jennings, 1977).
- *Adult occupational choices:* some occupations are almost entirely dominated by men. These include metalworking, weapon making, manufacture of musical instruments and the construction industries, such as boat building. The focus of these occupations is on creating systems (Geary, 1998).
- *Maths, physics and engineering:* these disciplines all require high systemising and are largely male dominated. The Scholastic Aptitude Math Test (SAT-M) is the mathematics part of the test administered nationally to college applicants in the US. Males on average score 50 points higher than females on this test (Benbow, 1988). Among individuals who score above 700, the sex ratio is 13:1 (men to women) (Geary, 1996).
- *Mechanics:* the Physical Prediction Questionnaire (PPQ) is based on an established method for selecting applicants to study engineering. The task involves predicting which direction levers will move when an internal mechanism of cogwheels and pulleys is engaged. Men score significantly higher on this test, compared with women (Baron-Cohen, forthcoming: 2007).

These results have obvious implications for social equality between men and women, and particularly for VOSS. If it can be shown that the majority of women are naturally inclined to behave quite differently from men, having different capabilities and interests, then it will be no surprise that men and women are segregated within the labour market and perhaps paid according to which skills are more prized by employers. For example, Baron-Cohen categorically states that we should not expect the sex ratio ever to be equal for certain types of job, like mathematicians or physicists. Indeed, the statistics set out in the Introduction show segregation in educational subjects and occupations that would coincide with these results to a substantial degree.

The performance of men and women in the fields of mathematics, physics, engineering and mechanics has been the subject of much debate recently, following the President of Harvard University, Larry Summers' statement, that the shortage of elite female scientists may reflect, in part, 'innate' differences between men and women (Summers, 2005). These comments caused great controversy in academia and beyond. Baron-Cohen's (2005) response was to agree with Summers on the one hand, that scientific aptitude is biologically weighted in favour of males. On the other hand, however, he argued that we should not presume a man necessarily would be the obvious choice at the appointment stage. This, he notes, would be unjustified discrimination. However, despite Baron-Cohen's desire to distance himself from theories such as Goldberg's Male Dominance Theory and establish a new agreeable face of evolutionary psychology across other disciplines, there are considerable similarities between the two approaches.

Spelke suggests with regard to Baron-Cohen's Empathising/ Systemising Theory that "it's an old idea, presented with some new language" (Spelke, in Pinker and Spelke 2005). Certainly Parsons (1942) argued that there are essentially two psychological traits – 'instrumental' and 'expressive' – which are the two sexual characteristics that correspond to 'male' and 'female' respectively. Spelke, despite being identified as a nativist (see Pinker and Spelke, 2005), maintains that the main causes of behavioural differences between men and women are social. Drawing on research on child development and aptitude comparisons since the 1970s, she asks "do we see sex differences?" and concludes quite simply that "the research gives us a clear answer to this question: we don't" (Spelke, in Pinker and Spelke, 2005). She goes on to explain:

> When you compare children's performance by sex, you see no hint of a superiority of males in constructing natural number concepts.…We are endowed with core knowledge systems that emerge prior to any formal instruction and that serve as a basis for mathematical thinking…. These systems develop equally in males and females. (Spelke, in Pinker and Spelke, 2005)

In terms of how these claims relate to occupational segregation, Spelke draws attention to the way in which Baron-Cohen labels occupations according to sex concentration and even stereotypes (despite his claims to the contrary), rather than to the nature of the work:

> … maybe the people who are better at mathematics are those who pursue more mathematically intensive careers. But this strategy raises two problems. First, which mathematically intensive jobs should we choose? If we choose engineering we will conclude that men are better at math because more men become engineers. If we choose

accounting, we will think that women are better at math because more women become accountants.... So which job are we to pick, to decide who has more mathematical talent? (Spelke, in Pinker and Spelke, 2005)

The particular experiments, listed earlier, which Baron-Cohen uses to illustrate his argument, do seem to chime with anecdotal examples of everyday life. However, these are *observations* rather than conclusive evidence of the causation of behaviour. This point is central to our understanding of the field. If we accept, for the moment at least, that women are in general better at sharing and turn taking and forging relationships and that men are more aggressive and naturally driven to establish a 'dominance hierarchy', it is quite easily argued that these may be manifestations of the ways in which individuals are socialised from birth along 'gender' lines. Similarly, sex differences in language and parenting styles could be learned rather than innate.

This is not to conclude there are no differences whatsoever between men and women in these domains. The counter-argument is rather that when considering the methodology of these tests (that is, behavioural observation), it is certainly difficult to ascertain that the causes of behavioural and consequently social differences between men and women are biological rather than social. Therefore, and crucially in terms of designing policy, we should be careful not to make that assumption when assessing occupational sex segregation.

Gilligan and Different Voice Thesis

Although Gilligan is unlikely to locate herself in the same camp as Goldberg and Baron-Cohen, her work may be seen to contain similar binary claims. In her seminal work on psychological development, *In a different voice*, Gilligan (1982/93) famously posits qualitative personality differences between men and women and argues that the sexes have different moral 'voices'. She describes men as more individualistic, achievement-oriented and motivated towards gaining power than women. In contrast, she argues, women are more selfless and concerned with the needs of others than are men and that it is the female voice that is systematically silenced. Women are disempowered when supposed 'universal' norms and stages of development are drawn from what actually are 'male' psychological tendencies (Gilligan, 1982/93, p 168).

Gilligan claims that there is a 'gendered dichotomy' of moral codes or primary concerns. She argues that men possess a morality of rights and formal reasoning, which she defines as the 'justice perspective'. This is distinguishable from the morality of care and responsibility, the 'care perspective', primarily associated with women. These two domains of moral concern, she suggests, are linked empirically to behavioural differences between men and women in social contexts. Gilligan contends that the (male) justice perspective is considered to be of greater social value than the (female) care perspective. In this sense, female traits are often "associated with personal vulnerability in the form of economic disadvantage" (Gilligan, 1987, p 32) and can be linked to the sexual division of labour both in terms of horizontal and vertical sex segregation in the labour market and in the division of labour between market and unpaid domestic work.

Gilligan should be commended for challenging Freudian ideas regarding female inferiority in the moral realm, and for recognising women as moral agents. Nevertheless, her analysis has a number of limitations. Faludi (1992), for example, argues that Gilligan's findings are weakened by the choice of case studies. The first study was based on a sample of eight boys and eight girls, and focused on two 11-year-olds whom she called Jake and Amy. The second study was restricted to 25 Harvard students, "hardly a representative slice of American society" (Faludi, 1992, p 363). The third study examined 29 young women's decisions not to have an abortion. Faludi points out that Gilligan's choice of case study here is highly problematic, since there can be no comparable male control group and describes it as "self-defeating in a book that supposedly examines the different ways men and women approach moral dilemmas" (Faludi, 1992, p 364)[2]. Furthermore, Connell (1987) argues that built in to the very design and interpretation of many of the studies that support binary models are cultural biases about stereotypical sex roles, which often result in misrepresentations of behavioural patterns (for similar arguments to Connell, 1987, see Sayers, 1982; Bleier, 1984).

It is not completely clear in Gilligan's work what the causes are of the two distinctive moral codes. Yet the supposition that they are to be expected as the social norm provides similar conclusions to the other binary-based arguments. The effects of socialisation may well contribute to many people's choice of occupation that match gender expectations. However, socialisation may also take the form of any number of a large plurality of motives, for example, tradition, family influence and adherence to societal norms, which should not be understood as women and men being divided into two different types of moral agency. Such a thesis negates the complexity of individual behaviour. As Connell emphasises, the hypothesis that there are some innate psychological differences between men and women cannot be ruled out but, even if they do exist and are not the result of socialisation, "they pale into insignificance beside the common capacities of women and men" (Connell, 1987, p 71).

Gilligan states that her work is "not characterised by gender", rather "the contrasts between male and female voices are presented ... to highlight a distinction between two modes of thought and to focus a problem of interpretation rather than to represent a generalisation about either sex" (Gilligan, 1982/93, p 67). Yet the reader cannot help but identify generalisations about the suggested distinct moralities of men and women in her work. Tong, for example, understands Gilligan to be implying "that *men* focus on rights, claims, self-interested demands, strict duties and obligations, burdens and limits on autonomy and that *women* focus on responsibilities to respond empathetically, to show concern in close relations, and to nurture and give aid" (Tong, 1997, p 166; for similar criticisms, see also Treadwell, 1987; Beutel and Marini, 1995).

Rosenberg (1982) investigated an extensive range of literature that posited a binary conception of 'character'. While she does not deny that society is often structured around a notion of sex difference, she concludes that the main finding over approximately 80 years of research is an overwhelming psychological *similarity* between men and women in the populations studied by psychologists. This conclusion is consistent with the findings of several contemporary psychological studies (see, for example, Tavris, 1992; Beal, 1994; Wark and Krebs, 1996; Spelke, in Pinker and Spelke, 2005).

Overall, then, we have seen that although the theories of Goldberg, Baron-Cohen and Gilligan make use of very different empirical research, there are notable similarities in their conclusions. All three interpret certain observations of social sex differences as reflections of ingrained, universal and, to variable degrees, predictable behavioural traits. For Goldberg and Baron-Cohen, these are straightforwardly biological for the average person. Analysis of Gilligan's work is slightly more complicated in that the causes of difference are not explicit. However, what we can infer from her work is the claim that men and women are different to the extent of moral conduct. As we shall examine subsequently, the ramifications of Gilligan's research are demands that we design society along binary lines to a considerable degree in order to counter sex inequality. For if men and women have distinguishable moral codes, then the vast majority of current 'mono social and institutional practices', using the male as their model of the individual, discriminates against women. This is a step that goes way beyond the recognition of the effects of socialisation and it is in this sense that she joins the binary-based theorists in this analysis.

Theories of patriarchy

The 'patriarchal subjugation of women' was a crucial assertion of the radicalising second-wave feminist movement that finally mobilised western states to introduce anti-discrimination laws in the early 1970s. Although theories of patriarchy feature less directly in political debates about sex inequality than they did between the 1970s and mid-1990s, they remain the rationale underlying our current anti-discrimination legislation.

The following exponents of Patriarchy Theory are Walby, who focuses on the historical evolution of patriarchy and asserts its continued malign presence having adapted to social change and Bryson, who calls for Patriarchy Theory's reinstatement as a major analytical tool in order to combat sex inequality in the context of liberal rights hegemony.

Walby and the patriarchy project

Walby (1986, 1990, 1997) rejects the claim that the generally lower position of women in the labour market reflects innate differences or moral predispositions (see also Hartmann, 1982). Rather, she argues that the historical and social context in which men have systematically excluded women from higher paying occupations in the labour market are the root cause of VOSS (see also Shorter, 1976; Cockburn, 1983; Delphy, 1984). As Walby states:

> I dispute the theories of those who argue that it is women's positions in the family which leads them to choose a lesser form of engagement in paid work than men. Rather the issue is, why do women suffer such appalling conditions of work in the family as many do? Why do most women marry on such terms? The answer is that the options for most women in paid work are not much better, because men have usually been successful in excluding women from the better work. (Walby, 1986, p 248)

Walby claims that men collectively have organised exclusionary practices and structures ('patriarchy')[3], which result in the inferior employment status of women. At the same time, there has been a construction and dissemination of a male breadwinner ideology, in which men's primary responsibility is labour market specialisation; women's, domestic work. Despite acknowledging the socioeconomic convergence between men and women, illustrated by the economic activity rates set out in the Introduction, Walby suggests that patriarchal forces have successfully survived and remain the major cause of VOSS in contemporary society.

She describes "a system of social structures in which men dominate, oppress and exploit women" (Walby, 1990, p 20). Reviewing the historical emergence of a patriarchal employment structure, Walby asserts that the development of capitalism and the expansion of wage labour might have offered women the opportunity to attain economic independence (see also Shorter, 1976). Instead, however, patriarchal strategies constructed by men have served to hinder women's economic advancement[4].

Walby (1990, 1997) suggests that there are two historically distinct patriarchal strategies, which enabled men to secure the better-paid jobs for themselves while maintaining their 'use' of women as primary domestic workers in the home[5]. She claims that the first of these strategies was that of exclusion, whereby women were 'blocked' from working in certain jobs and sectors. Examples include professions such as architecture, medicine, finance and law; skilled craft occupations; and industries such as engineering and printing. Historically, women were prevented from obtaining apprenticeships and trade union membership, both of which were often vital credentials for many employment positions. She argues that the strategy of explicit exclusion was prominent in the 19th century, while the maintenance of VOSS is the more common patriarchal strategy in contemporary society. Walby claims that women have been confined to occupations with less pay and status by male strategic organisation. She discusses how, during women's increasing participation in the labour market due to the 'war effort' of 1940–45, the state, together with trade unions (both male-dominated institutions), supported patriarchal measures. Women were brought into sectors where previously there had been few (if any) women, such as engineering and finance, but were paid far less than the men who had held those positions before the Second World War. Additionally, the state provided childcare facilities on a temporary basis and what were know as 'British Restaurants' offered subsidised meals for children of working mothers making work–life balance possible for the average family.

In the immediate postwar period, women were, often unwillingly, removed from many 'war effort occupations' and returned to the role of domestic worker, in order to re-establish the 'societal norm': a male breadwinner/female homemaker model. Accordingly, the provision of state childcare and subsidised meals ceased. Walby describes how these 're-normalising' policies had the effect of limiting employers' access to cheap female labour in a time of particular economic postwar boom and, as a result, ignited the mass expansion of part-time labour demand. This compromise between employers' needs for cheap labour and the demands of domesticity, sought to maintain women both in a servile role within the home and as secondary workers in the labour force. Patriarchy of this kind, she argues, remains the major source of female subordination in contemporary society.

The main argument then, is that during the 20th century the forces of patriarchy changed from being exclusively private (in that women were excluded from the labour market) to encompass the public workplace. In this sense, women, she claims, now have "the whole of society in which to roam and be exploited" (Walby, 1990, p 201).

Walby does acknowledge women's gains in academic qualifications and occupational status. However, she states that this "should not be interpreted as suggesting that ... patriarchy is over" (Walby, 1997, p 6). Rather, these developments have, ironically, contributed to the way in which patriarchy came to subsume both the domestic and the public (Walby, 1997, pp 22, 78).

In the domestic form the beneficiaries are primarily the individual husbands and fathers of the women in the household, while in the public form there is a more collective appropriation. In the domestic form the principal patriarchal strategy is exclusionary, excluding women from the public arena; in the public it is segregationist and subordinating (Walby, 1997, p 6).

However, while the stereotypes of sex roles were traditionally more rigid than in contemporary society, perceptions of women by *both* sexes have changed dramatically. It may be argued, then, that the assumption of a 'them and us' dynamic between men and women – as illustrated in Walby's research – is not consistent with the recognition and pursuit of attitudinal change towards sex roles[6]. While women have been, and continue to be, subordinated or exploited in various contexts, it is not *only* men who have perceived women in stereotypical terms. Women themselves also have perpetuated social norms of gendered behaviour, a fact that Walby fails to recognise (see, for example, Andelin, 1965).

Furthermore, Walby's theory of patriarchy does not address some of the more recent changes in the labour market, which have had adverse effects on men. For example, the de-industrialisation policies of the consecutive Conservative governments during the 1980s and 1990s heralded mass male unemployment due to closure or downsizing of companies such as British Steel, and industries such as shipbuilding and chemicals. As a result of high male unemployment in these types of male-dominated industries, the female-dominated service industries became the main source of income for the majority of households. Indeed, from the late 1990s onwards, women were often found to be the primary 'breadwinner' in many households. "According to government figures ... Middlesbrough ranks the highest in the league of significant industrial towns and cities in terms of the proportion of its workforce that is female" (*The Guardian*, 8 August 1998; 55.27% of Middlesbrough's total workforce is female). Similar female dominance in the labour force was found in Liverpool (54.5%), Glasgow (51.5%), Bristol (51.3%), Manchester (51.5%) and Sheffield (50.8%). Walby's thesis would seem to imply that men would prefer to be employed in the service industries, for example, rather than being dependent on unemployment benefit. More generally, as we shall see in the case of the BBC, there are many jobs that are both male dominated *and* among the lowest paid; again, Patriarchy Theory cannot make sense of such instances.

Moreover, it should not be assumed that all women who stay at home to perform domestic duties, who work part time and/or have low-status jobs, are 'subordinated'. Walby leaves little room for women's choice in her theory. Charles and Kerr (1988) and Pahl (1989) illustrate how often there is a system of 'pooling' income between men and women in households organised on an egalitarian basis. And although some jobs are not well paid in relative terms (for example, nurses or dancers), there may have been a conscious decision to pursue employment in these professions because of occupational preference rather than the pursuit of higher earnings.

Overall, while the form of feminism that Walby represents has been paramount in politicising the generally lower socioeconomic status of women, it would appear that there is a tendency within her account to over-emphasise *conscious* male dominance. As Fredman points out, "many men find themselves in positions of power or privilege in respect to women, rather than choosing to be there" (Fredman, 1997, p 2). Similarly, as Connell illustrates, "there are some groups of men who can recognise injustice when they see it and are far from comfortable with the position they have inherited" (Connell, 1987, p xi). Although societies and institutions may be *patriarchal* in that they are male dominated at the higher status levels, it does not necessarily follow that all those men have systematically and consciously organised themselves in order to deliberately subordinate their female colleagues; that is, not all patriarchal contexts constitute examples of *patriarchal strategy*. Walby seems to refer to the exploitative interests of patriarchy as if these form an unwritten code of conduct for all men. Pollert (1996) suggests that Walby tends to speak of patriarchy and capitalism as if they were actual entities, independent of real individuals. Pilcher (1999) similarly argues that Walby under-emphasises individual (or group) agency and over-emphasises patriarchal structures. Overall, Walby's Patriarchy Theory serves to legitimise stereotypical sex roles by effectively treating women and men as two distinct and homogeneous groups, and this is unlikely to help us understand the complexities of a highly diverse 21st-century workforce.

Bryson and re-conceptualised patriarchy

Bryson (forthcoming: 2007) has recently advocated a more moderate version of Patriarchy Theory. She recognises that the concept of patriarchy, as defined by Walby among others, has rather too many shortcomings to be a useful analytical device. Instead of defining patriarchy as a conscious collective project on the part of men to subordinate women, she wishes to use it as a tool for describing inequality between the sexes. Her main argument is that the largely unchallenged, hegemonic liberal rights discourse in western democracies has obscured the dominance of patriarchy and its discriminatory repercussions. Theorising from a Marxist perspective, Bryson contends that it is all too easy to be seduced by the idea that, because social and economic sex differences are set against a backdrop of equal rights, any inequalities between the sexes are a consequence of choice or merit and can thus be justified accordingly. Bryson argues that it is only by viewing liberal legal and political structures through the lens of patriarchy that we are able to recognise how the very structures of our society in fact contribute to, and perpetuate, the subordination of women, even if unwittingly.

Bryson refers to the equal rights doctrine, with irony, as 'common sense', which she claims is the dominant doctrine in liberal democracies. 'Common sense' renders people incapable of acknowledging societal inequality and discrimination. People, she argues, do not 'see' the patterns of injustice that are produced and reproduced by social and political institutions because they believe that western citizens live in a context of individual rights that proffer protection against discrimination and substantive choice of lifestyle. Bryson maintains, for example, that laws and welfare policies, based on liberal ideals, are, in fact, androcentric. By this she means that the laws and policies are modelled on a notion of the 'individual' that draws exclusively on 'male norms' and experiences; hence, under the guise of universal applicability, they neglect the needs, claims and entitlements of women.

While Bryson avoids some of the more rudimentary elements of standard patriarchy theories of sex inequality, her thesis does nevertheless contain several problematic suppositions. It may well be the case that the notion of the 'individual' in western laws and policies is more likely to resemble the traditional profile of a man than a woman. There are, however, some important laws, such as the right to paid leave for the purposes of parenting, which are heavily weighted in favour of women, irrespective of personal preferences. This, it will be argued later, is fundamentally detrimental to sex equality both on normative and practical grounds. Bearing in mind such an example, it is unhelpful to consider all liberal legal frameworks as androcentric. It is far more useful to consider the individual in non-stereotypical terms set against particular anachronistic institutional practices, for example, and this is unlikely to be achieved using a concept such as patriarchy, which *itself* presents a stereotypical account of behaviour.

Human capital-based theories

Human capital-based theories are increasingly used to explain the persistent pay gap between men and women. Many theorists are substituting claims of female choice in a new era of employment and lifestyle opportunities for traditional emphases on institutional bias, employer discrimination and policy shortcomings. Becker's Rational Choice Theory, for which he received the Nobel Prize in 1992[7], argues that a certain deficit in women's earnings is to be expected due to an economically rational decision on the part of familial households. Hakim's more recent Preference Theory (see, for example, 1996, 1998, forthcoming: 2007), is a development of Becker's thesis and claims that a shift in lifestyle choices available to women for the first time in the 21st century, provides an explanation as to why we should abandon the political objective of equalising average earnings between men and women.

Becker and Rational Choice Theory

Becker (1981/91) proposes that VOSS is primarily the result of rational choices made by men and women according to their human capital levels. Human capital in this context means education, accumulated employment experience and skills. Becker argues that, in general, women's human capital is negatively affected by their social expectation of being primarily responsible for domesticity and childcare, so that accumulatively they have less to offer the labour market than men. Drawing on classic human capital theories (see, for example, Mincer, 1966; Polacheck, 1981), he claims that "a sizeable [pay] gap is expected when women have specialised in household activities, have invested little in market human capital, and have allocated most of their energy to the household" (Becker, 1981/91, p 4). Becker goes on to argue therefore, that it makes sense (there is a rational decision) to consider the imbalance of human capital between men and women when individuals are organising their lifestyles efficiently.

Within his account, most men specialise more in paid work and women specialise more in domesticity; the result is a mutually advantageous arrangement between couples and families, based on the assumption that "altruism dominates family behaviour" (Becker, 1981/91, p 303). He maintains that, "since an altruist and his beneficiaries maximise family income and do not shirk their responsibilities or otherwise increase their well-being at the expense of others, altruism encourages the division of labour and an efficient allocation of resources" (Becker, 1981/91, p 295). Furthermore, he suggests that the decreases in fertility rates are, primarily, a consequence of the concerted effort of parents to concentrate their time, effort and money on fewer children in the attempt to produce 'higher quality' offspring.

For those women who are part of a household and work in paid employment he argues that human capital 'inferiority' is likely. He suggests that women engage in jobs (part time or full time) that 'reflect' their lower human capital and/or choose roles that are less demanding. These types of job, in turn, do not increase women's human capital level to the same degree as that of men (on the whole) and they are therefore less productive and are accordingly paid less. Because women choose lower status jobs with, for example, lower levels of skill than men, they are able to maintain more 'energy' for the unpaid duties within the home, which remain largely their responsibility, regardless of any role they may have outside the home:

> I show that married women with responsibility for childcare
> and other housework earn less than men, choose 'segregated'
> jobs and occupations, and invest less in market human capital
> even when married men and women work the same
> number of market hours. (Becker, 1981/91, p 57)

According to Becker, any differences between men and women can result, over a period of time, in very different relationships to the labour market. For example, the fact that only women can bear children leads women (far more than men) to anticipate the demands of childcare, which is likely to cause extensive sexual division of labour in the longer term. Even for those who are single and without children, Becker predicts that:

> Since single persons anticipate marriage and the sexual division of labour of married persons, single working men are likely to be more specialised toward the market sector than single working women. (Becker, 1981/91, p 41)

Becker holds up the nuclear family, organised by sex-role specialisation, as a societal ideal and (much like Goldberg) regards it as highly efficient. The nuclear family is used as the primary model for analysis throughout Becker's thesis, as it is the most common form of familial structure; hence, he suggests, it is in keeping with most people's lifestyle expectations. Although he refers to the changes in familial structure in recent decades, he does so primarily in the context of explaining how and why women's increased earning ability has been detrimental to the traditional nuclear family structure:

> [There is] no doubt that the family changed dramatically after the Second World War.... From 1950 to 1977 the legitimate birth rate declined by about one-third, the divorce rate more than doubled, the labour force participation rate of married women with young children more than tripled, and the percent of households headed by women with dependent children also almost tripled.... I believe that the major cause of these changes is the growth in the earning power of women. (Becker, 1981/91, p 350)[8]

He goes on to explain:

> Women with higher earnings gain less from marriage than other women do because higher earnings reduce the demand for children and the advantages of the sexual division of labour in marriage. Therefore women with higher earnings should be more prone to divorce.... Indeed, growth in the earnings of women during the last 30 years

has been a major cause (and a result) of the growth in divorce rates during this period. (Becker, 1981/91, p 336)[9]

However, while Becker's arguments may reflect the lifestyles and economic activities of some women, they do not provide a comprehensive explanation of VOSS.

For Becker, women with children have lower productivity levels within employment (due to the strategy of reserving energy for childcare duties within the home), have invested less in their human capital, and are paid accordingly. Several studies have pointed to the fact that women who take lengthy periods out of paid employment due to childcare tend to have lower levels of employment skills than workers with more consistent work histories (see, for example, Burchell and Rubery, 1990; Joshi and Paci, 1998). However, as Joshi and Paci conclude from their extensive research of women's pay, "it would be wrong to presume that motherhood necessarily lowers a woman's capacity for paid work" (Joshi and Paci, 1998, p 127). In a study of full-time working women, they compare mothers who return to work after a standard period of maternity leave ('maternity leavers') with childless women ('non-mothers') who also are working full time. They find that those maternity leavers were *not* penalised in terms of pay in comparison to non-mothers (Joshi and Paci, 1998, p 122)[10]. These results are consistent with the findings of several other studies (see, for example, England, 1984; Waldfogel, 1993, 1995). Hence, it is problematic to maintain (as does Becker) that all mothers positively *choose* low-paid 'female occupations' because these would penalise them less harshly for a period out of the labour market. This is a different claim to that of adaptive preferences. Becker asserts occupational choice is a conscious one made by women who prefer to reserve their energy for home life and so it makes sense for them to choose lower status jobs.

Becker also argues that single and childless women anticipate the sexual division of labour in their future lives; therefore they are inclined to invest less than men in their human capital, which in turn reduces their productive capacities. This claim is challenged by the findings of several studies, such as an ICM Research Survey (1996) that questioned young women on their life priorities. The rankings, in order of priority, were as follows: first, gaining a substantial income; second, travelling; third, maintaining a stable relationship; fourth, having a successful career. Notably, having children was ranked fifth. These results are consistent with a survey conducted by the National Council of Women (1992), which reported that only 13% of women of childbearing age thought that childbearing was necessary for 'life fulfilment'.

Furthermore, as many researchers point out, labour markets are not 'pure' or 'perfect'. Workers' remuneration is not necessarily proportionate to their human capital or productivity levels (see, for example, Craig et al, 1982; Burchell and Rubery, 1990; Corti and Dex, 1995). Moreover, and perhaps most importantly, Becker's approach leaves little room for the assessment of other factors that may contribute to VOSS, such as the stereotypes that he promotes and the status quo inequalities that he effectively serves to justify.

Also controversial is Becker's assertion that the sexual division of labour reflects 'altruism within the family', whereby it makes sense for the woman to concentrate her efforts in the home on small numbers of 'higher quality' children. Conversely, it could be argued that a woman's increased income earning ability may provide families with greater resources to produce more children, not less. It might also be the case that a *lower* income reduces the demand for children[11]. Even so, the economic determinism of these accounts lacks plausibility. Becker assumes that to marry and to have children are rational, economic decisions, neglecting the effects of the wide array of personal feelings, often neither economically related nor rational, that more commonly are associated with domestic affairs.

There are also problems with Becker's assumption that women's increased earning power is detrimental to the nuclear family structure and his claim that an increase in women's earning ability corresponds to an increase in divorce rates. As Maclean points out, "the evidence describing the adverse economic circumstances of the British mother-headed family after divorce is now overwhelming" (Maclean, 1991, p 21). Thus the evidence does not support Becker's equation of an increase of single mothers with the 'growth in the earning power of women' (see the figures on single-parent families in the Introduction and Moss et al, 1999).

Overall, Becker's Rational Choice Theory overlooks the complex factors that contribute to decision making, and suffers from the circularity of its central argument: that women earn less in the labour market because they have lower human capital and that this can be proved by the fact that they are paid less. As Felstead et al (2000) make clear, men earn considerably more than women, even when the skill content of both sexes occupations' are comparable (see also Joshi and Paci, 1998). This would suggest that VOSS would exist *irrespective* of human capital levels. Indeed, it is vital to recognise that such misguided assumptions about women's capacity for paid work, together with persistent practical limitations on individuals' choice of occupation *themselves* have a negative impact on people's experience of the labour market, and represent a cause of VOSS.

Hakim and Preference Theory

Hakim's Preference Theory (see, for example, 1996, 1998, forthcoming: 2007) can be seen as a development of Becker's Rational Choice Theory. She has two main criticisms of Becker's thesis that are the source of her advance. The first is that Becker assumes that childcare is a major part of unpaid work in the home and that this inevitably leads to substantially lower female productivity and human capital levels. Yet, as Hakim notes, in the context of services such as state-funded healthcare and education provided by welfare institutions, and also with the increase in 'high-tech' time and labour-saving household products, childcare is less demanding than Becker suggests. This, she argues (even when considering Becker's notion that parents are having fewer but 'higher quality' children), is particularly pertinent in light of decreasing birth rates and the dramatic increase in mothers returning to work after childbirth.

By extension, Hakim's second criticism is that Becker's argument places too much emphasis on childcare and tends to assume a false homogeneity among all women with respect to childcare. Hakim, conversely, focuses on the *heterogeneity* of women's relationships to the labour market. She claims that her explanations of women's stratified presence within employment hierarchies and instances of labour market abstention provide a more nuanced view of VOSS than Becker's Rational Choice Theory.

Essentially like Becker's, Hakim's central argument is that women's experiences of paid work are largely the result of choices made by the women themselves. She maintains however, that women, more than men, have "genuine choices to make between different styles of life", since men are more likely to be expected to work from the point of leaving full-time education to the point of retirement (Hakim, 1996, pp 207-8). These 'genuine choices' are the result of five social and economic changes that began, particularly in Britain and the US in the late 20th century, and are now, she argues, "producing a qualitatively different scenario of options and opportunities for women at the start of the 21st century". The five conditions as set out by Hakim are as follows (Hakim, forthcoming; 2007):

- the contraceptive revolution, which, from the 1960s onwards, gave sexually active women reliable and *independent* control over their own fertility for the first time in history;
- the equal opportunities revolution, which ensured that for the first time in history women obtained the right to enter all positions, occupations and careers in the labour market. Sometimes, this was extended to posts in the public sphere more generally. In some countries, legislation prohibiting sex discrimination goes much wider than just the labour market, giving women equal access to housing, financial services and other public services;
- the expansion of white-collar occupations, which are far more attractive to women that most blue-collar occupations;
- the creation of jobs for secondary earners, people who do not want to give priority to paid work at the expense of other life interests; and
- the increasing importance of attitudes, values and personal preferences in the lifestyle choices of people in prosperous, liberal modern societies.

The consequences of these relatively recent transitions has been the evolution of three types of women, each with different lifestyle preferences.

The first is the 'home-centred' category, said to represent between 10%-30% of women. Hakim contends that these women are more likely to concentrate on rearing children rather than undertaking paid work in the labour market, an option very seldom available to men. As she points out, "women may take refuge ... in the alternative identity and social role of housewife or mother, but this is not possible for men" (Hakim, 1996, p 209). Hakim suggests that any qualifications acquired by women in this group are not sought primarily for employment purposes; rather they are obtained so as to meet and attract males of the appropriate calibre. For example, to marry a male university graduate might be considered more likely to result in economic security.

Next is the 'adaptive' category, which, according to Hakim, comprises the greatest proportion of women (between 40%-80%). These women are those who "prefer to combine employment and family work without giving a fixed priority to either. They want to enjoy the best of both worlds" (Hakim, forthcoming; 2007). Hakim, like Becker, claims that many of these women will choose certain occupations that will facilitate more of a work–family balance. Also these women are most likely to work part time thereby splitting their time between home and employment. In earlier writings Hakim identified a sub-group of this category that she called the 'drifters'. She says of them that they:

> ... hang loose and refuse to choose fixed objectives, drifting with events and opportunities as they arise, pretending they can keep all their options open by refusing to close the door on any of them. This itself is an important choice, one men do not have, even if it is a poor one, leading to chaotically unplanned careers. (Hakim, 1996, p 208)

Hakim goes on to suggest that women in the adaptive category "fail to utilise any qualifications they may have, choose jobs for their convenience factors and social interest rather than a view to a long-term career, are concentrated in female occupations and have lower earnings" (Hakim, 1996, p 208).

Finally there are the 'work-centred' women who represent between 10%-30% of women and are predominantly focused on their careers. Hakim argues that these women's "family life is fitted around their work, and many of these women remain childless, even when married. Qualifications and training are obtained as a career investment rather than as an insurance policy, as in the adaptive group" (Hakim, forthcoming: 2007). They are, she argues, "as ambitious and determined as men, are concentrated in integrated or male-dominated occupations and have high earnings" (Hakim, 1996, p 209).

These three categories, Hakim maintains, illustrate the heterogeneity of women that is reflected in the labour market. She, like Becker, assumes that the lower employment status of the majority of women ('adaptives') is a reflection of their lower human capital and productivity levels.

Although Hakim recognises the existence of discriminatory practices towards women, she argues that:

> ... the current focus on low earnings as an indicator of discrimination has distracted attention from the fact that career women confront far more discrimination than secondary workers because they compete as equals with men but are often treated as uncommitted secondary earners. (Hakim, 1996, p 209)

Hakim claims that it is women's lack of collective 'solidarity' and ability to organise themselves (particularly among the largest class of women, in the adaptive category) that leads to a fracturing of female 'commitment' to paid work. This, in turn, largely explains women's generally (or in average terms) inferior position in the labour market:

> Male solidarity wins because women dither in their judgements, because they are swayed by the dominant male voice and also because women are divided in their preferences and interests. The key reason why male solidarity and male organisation are so effective is that women are diverse and divided. If men are the enemy, women make a hopeless adversary. (Hakim, 1996, pp 211-12)

A number of objections may be raised regarding the usefulness of Hakim's explanation of VOSS. While Hakim is right to acknowledge that for some women a well-paid job in the labour market is not more worthwhile or attractive than a lifestyle centred around the home or combining part-time work and childcare (a point often overlooked by patriarchy theorists), she pays insufficient attention to those who are not voluntary members, so to speak, of the home-centred or adaptive classes of women. Her theory offers little in the way of assessing the deficiencies of employment and domestic policy, both of which may impede women's capacity for paid work. Although Hakim claims to recognise the heterogeneity of women, it may be argued that by concentrating on women's preferences rather than including a sufficient assessment of restrictions on choice, she does not take account of the diverse experiences of women. In fact, she simply has three misleadingly homogeneous categories rather than just having one. As Crompton and Harris emphasise, "sociological explanations relating to women's employment patterns cannot rest upon a simplistic reduction to the argument that they are due to the fact that there are different 'types' of women" (Crompton and Harris, 1998, p 131).

Crompton and Harris draw comparisons between Hakim's Preference Theory and the debate surrounding the 'Orientations to Work Theory' in the 1960s and 1970s. Anticipating Hakim's theory (although usually focused on male employees), this theory sought to explain men's experience of stratification within the labour market by claiming that choices related to the extrinsic reward of pay represented the most important independent variable (see Goldthorpe et al, 1968). Hakim (1998) denies that Preference Theory is related to the orientations approach as she is concerned with different preferences, while the research of Goldthorpe et al focused on a single orientation. However, research by Blackburn and Mann (1979) has concluded that preferences are highly constrained by circumstances and so have a real, but very restricted, effect. As Crompton and Harris argue, criticisms of Goldthorpe et al's study also apply to Hakim's Preference Theory:

> Many workers were found to desire *both* extrinsic and intrinsic rewards from employment and thus no single 'orientation' could be identified (Hill, 1976, Blackburn and Mann, 1979)....More generally [it was argued that] studies of workers' attitudes had demonstrated that people have a tendency to adapt to what is realistically available for them and adjust to the realities of their employment situation (Blackburn and Mann, 1979)....Hakim's arguments ... focus on the significance of 'prior orientations' for women's employment patterns, and may be criticised in a similar fashion. (Crompton and Harris, 1998, p 123)[12]

On the one hand, then, Hakim appears to generalise that the majority of women are predisposed to a lack of commitment to employment (apart from the work-centred minority, who mirror the male role model). On the other hand, her account seems overly individualistic in the sense that she places too much emphasis on 'the female' as the chooser between each of these supposed categories (see also Fagan and Rubery, 1996, for further criticism).

Hakim offers some important criticisms of Becker's Rational Choice Theory. In so doing, she also illustrates very clearly how human capital-based arguments are reliant on binary-based views of the average man and woman. In discussing Becker's claims she states *why* it is that women 'choose' to adhere to sex roles – an unexplained tenet of his thesis:

> ... even childless women working full-time accept the sexual division of labour at home as efficient and give priority to their husband's careers, so children and their care are not an essential feature of the sexual division of labour at home, with its consequences for differential attainment [between men and women] in the labour market. (Hakim, 1996, p 210)

Binary-based theories such as Goldberg's or Baron-Cohen's fit well with the human capital-based theories first, as they offer to explain adherence to sex role specialisation and, second, to explain why, even when women are employed full time and without children, they are seen to fail to compete on an equal footing with men for the highest status occupations.

Hakim also, argues that Walby merely describes the mechanisms by which men discriminate against women but not the motives. Even Walby's most sophisticated account is essentially just 'description' (Hakim, 1996, p 210). Interestingly although patriarchy theorists deny biological roots to inequality it is not clear according to their view why *men* subjugate *women*. Hakim suggests that the answer is to be found in men's 'natural instinct' to compete successfully for the higher status occupations: "faced with a race, men run harder than women" (Hakim, 1996, p 210). In a similar vein, Hakim points out that theories of patriarchy fail to explain why it is that some male-dominated occupations can be lower paid than some female-dominated occupations. In answer to this theoretical shortcoming, Hakim states:

> Goldberg points out that if these theories [of patriarchy] were true, there would be no male-dominated occupations that paid substantially less than women's occupations.... Male roles are not high status because they are male, Goldberg argues. It is simply that *any* role that acquires high status (as indicated by high earnings) will attract more men than women, so will *become* male-dominated as a result of its position in the hierarchy. (Hakim, 1996, p 8)

Hakim offers this combination of theories as a comprehensive explanation both of women's heterogeneity and of VOSS within the labour market: "male patriarchal solidarity and male organisation to promote male interests are disproportionately successful because women are sharply divided in their objectives and fields of activity" (Hakim, 1996, p 212).

However, first, as illustrated earlier during the discussion of Becker's work, the argument that women's general lower labour market position is simply a reflection of their human capital and productivity levels provides a limited analysis of VOSS.

By referring to Male Dominance Theory as a possible explanation for the motivation for sex-role specialisation, Hakim makes the unwarranted assumption that all women seek and adhere to a gender stereotype. What is more, in her claim that Goldberg's theory explains male exclusionary practices (as described by Walby and Hartmann), it would appear that Hakim is making a similar assumption about men[13]. However, these assumptions are not consistent with the rest of her argument. In Hakim's conclusion, she states that "we need to know if the highest achievements are accessible to, even if restricted to, women following the male employment profile, or whether it takes a lot more than that to succeed in male dominated careers" (Hakim, 1996, p 215). Yet, if we accept the binary-based theories of male dominance, then there is little hope of combating VOSS.

In focusing only on work-centred women in the context of female disadvantage, Hakim appears to ignore the restrictive processes that limit the choices of women in the other two categories (home-centred and adaptive). More importantly, she (like Becker) does not account for the stark variations between women's socioeconomic circumstances and the ways in which these impact on individuals' choice of lifestyle and relationship to the labour market. The policy implications of the human capital-based arguments discussion will be discussed in further detail in subsequent chapters.

Conclusion

This chapter has emphasised the limitations of each of these theoretical approaches and has illustrated the ways in which each camp tends to assume a false homogeneity among women, irrespective of various claims to the contrary. All make the error, it is argued here, of assuming that general trends, such as women's overall lower labour market position, simply reflect certain predispositions to sex inequality. This is an assessment that ignores the heterogeneity of women *and* men, and the fundamental lack of options available to both sexes, a point to be explored in the following chapters. Moreover, there appear to be unwarranted elements of resignation in each of these accounts, such that, were their claims to be accepted, there would be little hope of identifying solutions to current patterns of vertical segregation.

Notes

[1] Pilcher (1999) goes on to challenge reductionist biological accounts by discussing how some people are born with indeterminate genitalia and are subsequently categorised as either female or male.

[2] Similarly Gilligan (1995) relies on a small study of 26 'at risk' girls from which to generalise about female psychology.

[3] Walby often uses 'gender regime' instead of 'patriarchy', but she considers the two terms to be synonymous (Walby, 1997, p 6).

[4] Although both writers are associated with the dual-systems theory (that is, the impact of both patriarchy and capitalism), it should be noted that Hartmann views capitalism and patriarchy as generally harmonious, whereas Walby considers them often to be conflicting; that is, that capitalism makes use of women as cheap labour whereas patriarchy perpetuates the role of women as unpaid domestic workers in the home. However, Walby still sees both systems as simultaneously restrictive for women.

[5] Walby is often considered to be developing Hartmann's Patriarchy Theory; see, for example, Hakim (1996); Crompton (1997); Pilcher (1999).

[6] Some feminist writers have been more extreme. For example, Greer writes that in the absence of an alternative to what she see as humiliation, social segregation is by far preferable (Greer, 1999).

[7] The Nobel Prize website states that Becker has "extended the domain of micro-economic analysis to a wide range of human behaviour and interaction, including non-market behaviour" (www.nobel.se/index.html).

[8] Becker is referring to figures that relate to the US in this example.

[9] Effectively Becker claims that there are two ways in which women aim to secure their income; namely, actual, or the expectation of, sex-role specialisation (incorporating marriage and children) or increased economic productivity and, by extension, earning ability (incompatible with marriage and children).

[10] Joshi and Paci also studied the pay levels of part-time work, which tended to be the lowest paid. Their conclusions were consistent with their study of full-time work: "what we have found – in common with other studies – is ample evidence of a [pay] 'penalty to part-time' whether or not a woman has children" (Joshi and Paci, 1998, p 177).

[11] Perhaps Becker's argument would be more relevant to an earlier context, when children were seen as a means of income (through child labour), prior to the introduction of pensions, sickness benefit and so on.

[12] The criticisms of Hakim's Preference Theory are supported in Crompton and Harris's (1998) research. However, it should be noted that Patriarchy

Theory (criticised here for its over-simplifying complex phenomena) is a major part of their explanation of VOSS.

[13] With regard to Hakim's support for Goldberg's argument that testosterone directly relates to social behaviour, it is interesting to note that she refers to the variation of testosterone levels between *men* as a "a finding which may help to explain male homosexuality" (Hakim, 1996, p 8). The implication is that the less testosterone a man has, the less prone he will be to an 'aggressive advantage', so the less likely it will be that he attains the highest status positions within hierarchies. However, as previously noted, there is no medical evidence to support this argument.

TWO

VOSS in the BBC

This chapter illustrates the major quantitative findings of a large and detailed empirical investigation of occupational sex segregation in the BBC. It is from these data that we can begin our empirical test of the causal explanations of VOSS contested in the previous chapter. First, we will take a brief look at the sex ratios in the BBC that provide optimal data from which to make comparisons of male and female workers across all sectors of the organisation. The sample is made up of 19,129 full-time workers employed within the BBC's 79 occupations. The split between the sexes is virtually even, with 49% of the total workforce female and 51% male. In Figure 1, all 79 occupations are ordered according to sex concentration, beginning with Job No 1 (code HRJ/personnel assistant: 98% female), through to Job No 79 (code BEL/technicians: 0% female). The data codes and percentages appear in Table 1, and the full dataset in Appendix 2.

These data show us that there is a full spectrum of sex concentrations, from highly female-dominated occupations (predominantly dark grey in Figure 1), through a middle section with a more even spread of both male and female employees (dark grey and light grey), to highly male-dominated occupations (predominantly light grey). This is a clear example of overall occupational sex segregation – the tendency for

Figure 1: Concentration of full-time working women and men in each BBC occupational group

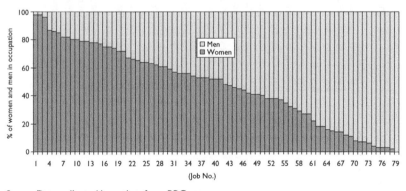

Source: Data collected by author from BBC resources

Table 1: BBC jobs by female percentage

Job no	Code	Typical job	% female	Job no	Code	Typical job	% female
1	HRJ	Personnel assistant	98	25	FMT	Premises operations	66
2	SFP	Personal assistant	98	26	NJF	Head of language section	65
3	SFQ	Secretary	97	27	TPG	Department management	63
4	HRT	Personnel officer	87	28	FMS	Reprographic worker	63
5	RPC	Radio production support	86	29	TPR	Script editor	62
6	FFR	Finance assistant	86	30	TPP	Floor/stage management	59
7	TPC	Tele production support	83	31	LRS	Professional librarian	59
8	ASQ	Allocations support	82	32	PMX	Viewer/listener relation	58
9	ASP	Management assistant	81	33	PMM	Press/publicity manager	57
10	OPJ	Resources man'gt support	81	34	PMW	Sales/marketing	57
11	PMU	Press/publicity officer	80	36	OPE	Resources coordinator	56
12	NJC	News research	80	37	TPB	Television producer	55
13	ASE	Scheduling assistant	79	38	LRP	Library services	54
14	FMQ	Facilities support	78	39	EST	Trainer	53
15	NJT	Teletext/subtitling	78	40	RPB	Radio producer	52
16	TDP	Costume	78	41	NJD	News presentation	52
17	TPE	Tele plan coordination	77	42	RPD	Radio producer	48
18	PMV	Publicity specialist	76	43	TPA	Tele editorial staff	48
19	LFJ	Legal support	75	44	FFP	Business manager	47
20	LFP	Contracts/negotiations	73	45	RPA	Radio editorial staff	45
21	TPQ	Programme finance	72	46	NJR	Journalist	44
22	PMF	Chief publicity officer	69	47	TPM	Tele management	44
23	CSR	Channel management	67	48	TPD	Tele presentation	41
24	FFK	Finance support	67	49	RPM	Radio management	41

Table 1: BBC jobs by female percentage **contd.../**

Job no	Code	Typical job	% female	Job no	Code	Typical job	% female
50	FFM	Finance management	40	**65**	BEK	Br'cast eng tech sup	16
51	FFF	Man'gt accountant	39	**66**	OPM	Operations manager	14
52	NJB	News producers	38	**67**	OPQ	Lighting	14
53	CSM	Commission' management	38	**68**	OPW	Technical operator	13
54	TDQ	Graphics	37	**69**	AST	Storekeeper	11
55	NJA	News editorial	35	**70**	OPP	Camera person	8
56	TDU	Scenic design	33	**71**	BEP	Com. Engineer	7
57	ITQ	IT devel'pt/anal	31	**72**	ITX	IT infrastructure	7
58	NJM	News manager	29	**73**	OPK	Rigger driver	6
59	FMM	Facilities management	28	**74**	GEW	Eng specialist	4
60	ITK	IT user support	27	**75**	BEQ	Maintenance engineer	3
61	ITF	IT management	22	**76**	TDK	Tele design op	3
62	OPU	Sound	18	**77**	BER	Installation engineer	3
63	OPS	Picture editing	18	**78**	BEM	Eng management	2
64	OPT	Post production	16	**79**	BEL	Technician	0

Source: Data collected by author from BBC resources

men and women to be employed in different occupations from each other across all occupations – and resembles the national data set out in Figure A of the Introduction. As explained in the Introduction, overall segregation is frequently confused with horizontal segregation. One of the purposes of this chapter is to clarify the distinctions between overall, horizontal and vertical segregation and as we go through the various stages of this quantitative examination these should become apparent. Having established the existence of overall segregation – in order to evaluate VOSS – the next stage is to assess the difference between the sexes with regard to pay grades.

BBC pay grades

All staff employed in the jobs under analysis are paid according to the BBC's pay grade system. In the absence of individual salaries, pay grades that are numerically progressive provide a hierarchical structure that will be used to devise a vertical scale of pay from which we can begin to detect VOSS. A complete list of pay grades, ranging from grade 1 (£10,740 to £15,540 per annum) to grade 12 (£198,001 and above per annum), appears in Appendix 3.

Figure 2 shows the percentage of all full-time working women and men in each of the 12 pay grades and here we can see a clear disparity between men and women's pay, indicating substantial degrees of VOSS.

Figure 2: Concentration of male and female employees within each BBC pay grade

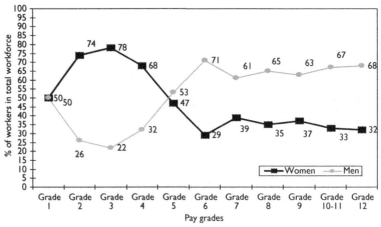

Source: Data collected by author from BBC resources

In the lowest paid jobs (pay grade 1) men and women are found in equal numbers. However, as the pay grades increase, women become over-represented in the lower grades (and men under-represented) until a 'cross over' point at pay grade 5, where men become over-represented in the higher grades and women conversely under-represented. Together these data produce a strong correlation between sex and pay – VOSS. Moreover, Figure 2 illustrates the inevitable symmetry of segregation extremely well (see the Introduction to this book).

From the full dataset in Appendix 2, it is possible to calculate the mean pay grade for each occupation and in this way we can see which occupational categories (particularly in terms of male and female concentration) are more likely to be better paid overall. The mean pay grade for each occupation is set out in Table 2.

Despite signs of strong correlations between sex and pay, there is, however, considerable variation in pay grades across jobs *irrespective* of male and female concentration. For example, the most highly female-concentrated occupation (Job No 1 with 98% females) has a mean pay grade of 3.6, and similarly the most highly male-concentrated occupation (Job No 79 with 0% females) has a mean pay grade of only 4.4. Irrespective of the fact that both jobs are relatively lowly paid, a comparison of the two shows very high levels of sex segregation but with little pay inequity between them. Thus, when calculating segregation and its composite dimensions (horizontal and vertical), the relationship of this particular pair of jobs would contribute a much higher degree of horizontal segregation than vertical. (The calculation of segregation and how the three types of segregation relate to each other will be detailed a little further on.) These data illustrate therefore that there is no straightforward correlation between high levels of male concentration and higher pay grades. That is to say, segregation per se is not a zero sum game between sex and pay, a point to which we will return later when considering the possible implications of these data in relation to political objectives and policy designs.

Table 2: Mean pay grades for all BBC occupations

Job no	Code	Number total staff	Number male	Number female	% female	Mean pay grade	Job no	Code	Number staff	Number male	Number female	% female	Mean pay grade
1	HRJ	50	1	49	98	3.6	25	FMT	169	58	111	66	2.3
2	SFP	92	2	90	98	3.5	26	NJF	52	18	34	65	8.7
3	SFQ	775	27	748	97	2.9	27	TPG	52	19	33	63	7.5
4	HRT	210	27	183	87	6.2	28	FMS	40	15	25	63	2.1
5	RPC	595	83	512	86	3.5	29	TPR	50	19	31	62	6
6	FFR	42	6	36	86	4	30	TPP	194	79	115	59	4.6
7	TPC	823	137	686	83	4.4	31	LRS	306	126	180	59	4.3
8	ASQ	50	9	41	82	3	32	PMX	62	26	36	58	3.9
9	ASP	730	140	590	81	2.9	33	PMM	68	29	39	57	10
10	OPJ	62	12	50	81	3.2	34	PMW	144	62	82	57	5.9
11	PMU	181	36	145	80	5.7	35	HRM	51	22	29	57	10.4
12	NJC	576	117	459	80	3.5	36	OPE	121	53	68	56	4.9
13	ASE	58	12	46	79	3.8	37	TPB	1,046	473	573	55	7.5
14	FMQ	120	26	94	78	2.3	38	LRP	304	141	163	54	3
15	NJT	78	17	61	78	5.3	39	EST	112	53	59	53	6.7
16	TDP	64	14	50	78	3.9	40	RPB	565	270	295	52	7.3
17	TPE	47	11	36	77	4.6	41	NJD	52	25	27	52	6.7
18	PMV	70	17	53	76	4.4	42	RPD	60	31	29	52	6.3
19	LFJ	79	20	59	75	4.2	43	TPA	148	77	71	48	9.5
20	LFP	153	42	111	73	6.3	44	FFP	154	82	72	48	7.4
21	TPQ	156	44	112	72	5.7	45	RPA	47	26	21	45	9.2
22	PMF	42	13	29	69	7.3	46	NJR	2,811	1,573	1,238	44	7
23	CSR	48	16	32	67	6.4	47	TPM	267	150	117	44	9.7
24	FFK	434	145	289	67	3.6	48	TPD	104	61	43	41	6.2

Table 2: Mean pay grades for all BBC occupations **contd.../**

Job no	Code	Number total staff	Number male	Number female	% female	Mean pay grade	Job no	Code	Number staff	Number male	Number female	% female	Mean pay grade
49	RPM	81	48	33	41	9.9	**65**	BEK	51	43	8	16	2.5
50	FFM	94	56	38	40	9.6	**66**	OPM	209	179	30	14	8.9
51	FFF	101	62	39	39	8.7	**67**	OPQ	208	179	29	14	5.2
52	NJB	545	337	208	38	7.3	**68**	OPW	189	165	24	13	5.9
53	CSM	42	26	16	38	11.2	**69**	AST	45	40	5	11	2.2
54	TDQ	233	146	87	37	6.8	**70**	OPP	326	300	26	8	6.2
55	NJA	561	365	196	35	8.6	**71**	BEP	168	156	12	7	6.4
56	TDU	40	27	13	33	7.3	**72**	ITX	57	53	4	7	7.5
57	ITQ	225	155	70	31	6.3	**73**	OPK	270	253	17	6	3.2
58	NJM	274	194	80	29	10.3	**74**	GEW	131	126	5	4	7.9
59	FMM	159	114	45	28	6.5	**75**	BEQ	590	570	20	3	6.4
60	ITK	110	80	30	27	4.5	**76**	TDK	97	94	3	3	4.1
61	ITF	72	56	16	22	8.5	**77**	BER	104	101	3	3	7.9
62	OPU	794	649	145	18	6	**78**	BEM	94	92	2	2	8.6
63	OPS	558	458	100	18	6.7	**79**	BEL	87	87	0	0	4.4
64	OPT	110	92	18	16	5.1							

Source: Data collected by author from BBC resources

Measurement of VOSS

To illustrate further the dimensions of segregation within the BBC, this section will set out the calculation of VOSS as a dimension of overall segregation according to the 'Cambridge approach'. This approach, pioneered by Robert Blackburn working with various research collaborators (see, for example, Blackburn et al, 2001) prescribes the Gini coefficient (G) for calculating overall segregation, and Somer's D (D) for the vertical dimension (using the data in Table 2)[1].

First we calculate overall occupational sex segregation using G, measuring the extent to which the proportions of male and female workers within the various occupations depart from their proportions within the workforce as a whole (49% female and 51% male); in other words, the extent to which occupations are 'male' or 'female'. G takes a value from 0 (which represents zero segregation) to 1 (which is total segregation). Thus, the higher the value of the coefficient, the higher the level of overall occupational sex segregation.

The Gini coefficient is expressed as the following formula:

$$G = 1/MF \ S \ i < j \ (FiMj - FjMi)$$

In this formula, Mi and Fj represent respectively the numbers of men in job i and women in job j, and so $Mi + Fi = Ni$ which is the total number of employees in job i. Note that the jobs are ordered by the proportion (or concentration) of women in each job, so that whenever $i < j$ we have $Fi/(Mi + Fi) > Fj/(Mj+Fj)$ or, equivalently $(FiMj - FjMi) > 0$. M and F denote the total number of men and women in the workforce.

As with Figure 1, the measurement of sex concentration in each occupation does not, in itself, tell us anything about pay inequities; rather, it only illustrates the distribution of sexes across occupations. To measure the vertical dimension, we apply Somer's D. Somer's D is a measurement of segregation, which correlates the ordering of occupations by sex with the ordering by an ordinal scale – in this case the BBC's 12 pay grades.

Somer's D can be expressed by the following formula:

$$D = 1/MF \ (|P| - |Q|)$$

According to this method, a pair of jobs (i, j) is correlated if job i is worse paid than job j. Otherwise, the pair is said to be uncorrelated. And if a pair (i, j) is correlated, then (j, i) is uncorrelated. P and Q are the sets of all correlated and uncorrelated pairs respectively. $|P|$ is the total number of pairs of individual women and men, where their jobs constitute a correlated pair, and $(|Q|)$ uncorrelated.

D takes a value between $+1$ and -1, in which a positive value indicates that segregation is biased against women and a negative value indicates that segregation is biased against men. In a workforce where a higher concentration of men in a particular occupation *always* implies a higher rate of pay, both G and D would coincide (as positive values only) and we would conclude that *all* segregation was vertical. However, as previously noted, the true likeness of segregation displays some 'reverse segregation'; some male-dominated occupations are less well paid in comparison to some female-dominated occupations. Such instances (uncorrelated pairs) make a negative contribution towards the total value of D, thus creating a discrepancy between the final values of G and D. Indeed, the formula for D can be thought of as a sum of positive and negative terms, representing the components of segregation that are biased in favour of men and women respectively. G is the sum of the absolute values of these terms (that is, no negative or positive distinction is made, as there is no reference to the ordinal scale). In this way, in keeping with the normative understanding of segregation, we can deduce that overall segregation (as measured by G) is *not* equal to vertical segregation (as measured by D), thus leaving a 'remainder' that is expressed as 'horizontal segregation' (in this case, segregation without pay inequity). In order to generate a value for horizontal segregation for purposes of visualising the relationship between overall and vertical segregation (Figure 3), horizontal segregation can be deduced as the square root of overall^2 − vertical^2.

Figure 3: Full-time working women and men in the BBC

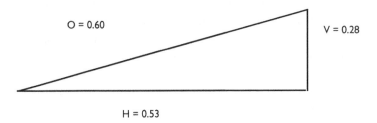

O = overall segregation, H = horizontal segregation, V = vertical segregation

Source: Data collected by author from BBC resources

Figure 3 provides yet another illustration of how vertical segregation falls far short of constituting all types of segregation in the workforce. VOSS is indeed a far more complex phenomenon than often perceived in studies and measurements of 'inequality'.

Generally speaking, the 'segregation triangle' shown here should be understood as the best representation of segregation, at least in all western liberal democracies, where large numbers of women and men are employed in labour markets not restricted by segregationist laws. Comparative measurements using the Cambridge approach have been administered to cross-national data. Consequently, each labour market analysis has produced varying degrees of both horizontal and vertical segregation (see Blackburn et al, 2001). Whether applied to organisational settings such as the BBC, or to national labour force data, it is possible to compare the pay gaps in this way, as the components of overall segregation: the higher the horizontal dimension, the lower the vertical dimension, the smaller the pay gap. For example, Sweden, perhaps not surprisingly given its famously egalitarian ethos, has a low vertical dimension and one of the lowest pay gaps in Europe despite relatively high levels of horizontal segregation. This study is the first to apply the Cambridge approach to an organisational setting and future research will enable cross-organisation and, in turn, cross-sector comparisons. In the absence of a similar study, some national data measurements, although not directly comparable (Blackburn et al, 1999a) can be tentatively compared to the BBC data. The UK data showed very similar amounts of VOSS for full-time working non-manual female workers and all non-manual male workers[2]. For overall segregation the value for the national data was 0.64, for the horizontal dimension the value was 0.58 and 0.27 for the vertical. In as much as a comparison can be made, these results would suggest that the progressive policies of the BBC have not had a dramatic effect on the vertical dimension of the occupational sex segregation within its labour force.

The Cambridge approach was employed here to determine the relationship between the two dimensions of segregation. Due to the significant level of horizontal segregation produced in this calculation we can verify that segregation patterns are far more complex than the common assumption that segregation is directly equivalent to pay inequities between the sexes. It is also possible, however, to scrutinise the data more closely.

'Female jobs', 'mixed jobs' and 'male jobs'

A limitation of measuring VOSS with statistics of association (which also applies to the Cambridge approach) is that it produces only a very general picture, lacking more specific comparative elements. Therefore, it is useful to distinguish between 'female', 'mixed' and 'male' occupational categories. These occupational categories are defined by creating a 10% margin either side of the female percentage of the total staff (49%). Hence, the 'mixed jobs' category comprises jobs in which the percentage of females is between (and inclusive of) 39% and 59%, producing a category that does not substantially deviate from the male/female concentration of the BBC's labour force as a whole. In this way, Jobs No 30 (59% females) to 51 (39% females) represent the 'mixed jobs' category; Jobs No 1 (98% females) to 29 (62% females) comprise the 'female jobs' category; and Jobs No 52 (38% females) to 79 (0% females) make up the 'male jobs' category, as illustrated in Figure 4.

Two main points of interest emerge in Figure 4. First, the BBC's labour force is divided almost completely equally between the three categories (31% 'female jobs'; 36% 'mixed jobs'; and 33% 'male jobs'), in stark contrast to the British labour market as a whole, where 'mixed' occupations only constitute approximately 16%. This is particularly important when we consider the second point, that the highest paid jobs are concentrated in the 'mixed jobs' category (albeit closely followed by the 'male jobs'). The concentration of the highest paid jobs in the 'mixed' category is a highly significant factor and cannot be deduced from the results of standard readings of segregation, which only give a crudely related set of aggregated values. Despite these

Figure 4: Mean pay grades of 'female', 'mixed' and 'male' jobs in the BBC (smoothed data)

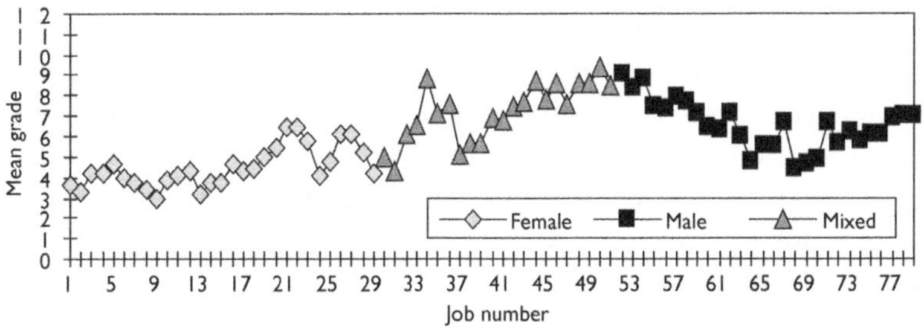

Source: Data collected by author from BBC resources

Figure 5: Percentage of male and female BBC employees by grade in 'female jobs'

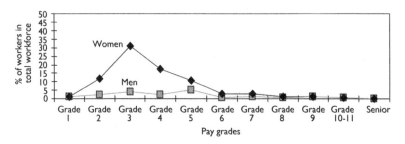

Source: Data collected by author from BBC resources

positive tendencies, however, it is also apparent that 'female jobs' (at an average of pay grade 3.9) are paid considerably less than both the 'male jobs' (average pay grade of 6.7) and the 'mixed jobs' (6.9).

Figure 5, which shows the proportion of men and women in 'female jobs' by pay grade, enables us to see another way in which VOSS manifests itself.

Women are over-represented in the lowest pay grades of 1 to 5. As the pay grades increase, the proportions of men and women converge, although it is important to emphasise that only 19% of the staff in 'female jobs' are men, compared to 81% women. Accordingly, these relatively few men are spread much more evenly across all pay grades and are proportionately more likely than the women to occupy the higher paid positions, while the women tend to be clustered in and around pay grade 3. To recall the types of jobs encountered in this category, the 10 jobs with the greatest concentration of female employees are personnel assistant, personal assistant, secretary, personnel officer, finance assistant, radio production support, television production support, allocations support, management assistant and press/publicity officer. These jobs, irrespective of the incumbent's sex, tend to be located in the mid to low pay grades (with the exception of personnel officers, where staff are distributed more evenly across the pay grades). In aggregate terms, the mean pay grade for women in these jobs is 3.8, compared to 4.5 for men and, as becomes apparent when comparing these data with the 'male jobs' and 'mixed jobs', the greatest pay gaps for *both* sexes are found between the 'female jobs' and the other two job categories.

Turning to the 'male jobs' in Figure 6, the concentration of women and men is precisely the reverse of that within the 'female jobs': 19% of staff are women and 81% male.

Figure 6: Percentage of male and female BBC employees by grade in 'male jobs'

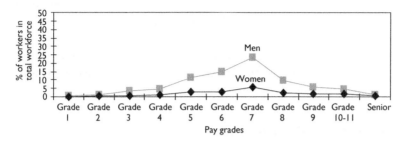

Source: Data collected by author from BBC resources

In the 'male jobs' category the pattern of distribution is somewhat surprising. Although, as might be anticipated, men predominate in all pay grades (with the majority situated in the middle pay grades of 5 to 9), women are relatively well represented across all the pay grades, with a slight clustering in pay grade 7, rather than in the lowest pay grades. In fact, the mean pay grade for women in 'male jobs' is 6.9, compared to 6.6 for men. This shows, perhaps counter-intuitively, that women are likely to fare well in male-dominated spheres; indeed, some of the highest paid women are employed in 'male jobs'. Such jobs, on the whole, tend to be of a much more technical nature, and include camera person, communications engineer, IT infrastructure staff, rigger driver, engineering specialist, maintenance engineer, tele design operative staff, installation engineer, engineering management and technician.

Lastly, in Figure 7 we turn to the 'mixed' category, which is made up of 49% females and 51% males (the same proportions as the entire BBC full-time working labour force).

Figure 7: Percentage of male and female BBC employees by grade in 'mixed jobs'

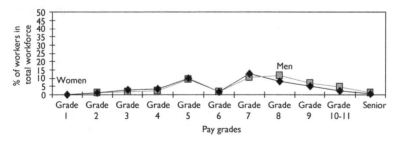

Source: Data collected by author from BBC resources

These data, markedly encouraging, show that women and men are very similarly distributed across all pay grades, with particular clustering in pay grades 7 and 8. Overall, the mean pay grade for women in these jobs is 6.6, compared to 7.2 for men. The types of jobs under analysis here are, for example, journalists and television producers and tend to be highly skilled[3]. Hence, despite overall levels of VOSS, in fact it is in the interests of the employee to work in mixed occupations as opposed to male-dominated occupations.

Preliminary observations

An in-depth causational analysis of VOSS is the subject of the following chapter in which the qualitative findings are presented. However, these rather striking data permit some preliminary observations about claims underpinning the various theoretical explanations addressed in the previous chapter.

This quantitative exercise aimed to illustrate the extent of vertical segregation within a large 'optimal conditions' employment context. Figure 1 indicated a high level of overall sex segregation across the 79 BBC occupations (reflecting a pattern familiar in the British labour market as a whole, as indicated in the Introduction). Figure 2 showed the acute tendency for men to be over-represented in the higher pay grades. Although, unfortunately, this result might be unsurprising considering the persistent national pay gap between men and women, it is disappointing in the context of a 'best case scenario', which has admirably attempted to eradicate any forms of sex bias. The Cambridge approach was employed to determine the relationship between the two dimensions of segregation. Due to the significant level of horizontal segregation produced in this calculation we could verify that segregation patterns are far more complex than the common assumption that segregation is directly equivalent to pay inequities between the sexes.

Consequently, on closer analysis, and testament to the fact that macro-aggregate studies are impoverished in their analysis of segregation patterns, the trends *within* sex concentrated occupations emerged not only as far more complex but also far more informative with regard to understanding average female disadvantage. In distinguishing between female-dominated jobs, male-dominated jobs, and 'mixed jobs', it was possible to show how women (albeit in small numbers) in fact were distributed across the 'male jobs' in similar numbers to men (with a particular concentration in pay grade 7) and, surprisingly, commanded a slightly higher average pay grade. A similarly encouraging result emerged from the 'mixed jobs' category, which contains the highest paid jobs at the BBC, where equal numbers of men and women were distributed across the pay grades. Only in the 'female jobs' category was there a significant drop in pay for women, who are concentrated around the low-paid grade 3, with men more evenly distributed across pay grades. The combination of these trends results in an overall, and severe, average disparity between the sexes. From this it is possible to deduce that the segregation between 'male' and 'mixed jobs' (see Table 1 for job names) is mostly horizontal, while the segregation between 'female jobs' and the other two categories is vertical.

Disaggregating the data in this way contributes to a heightened appreciation of the potential for greater equality between the sexes. Even at this stage in the investigation it would appear that ethos, environment and opportunity of a particular kind all play stronger roles in the formation of segregation patterns than has been recognised by the various causal theories previously discussed. Evidently it is occupation and not sex that determines pay (otherwise there would be much stronger vertical trends within these data). Consequently, attention should be directed at the reasons why individuals find themselves in a particular occupation. If we assume from these data that innate differences between men and women are not the primary reason for commanding a particular level of pay, then we are compelled to make a distinction between genuine preferences on the one hand, and available choices on the other. This, as will be seen in the following chapters, in fact results in a major departure from the prevalent causal theories of VOSS; patriarchy theories, binary-based theories and human capital-based theories (namely Rational Choice and Preference Theory).

For example, in very elementary terms, the very fact that women (while in the minority) command, on average, better pay levels within the 'male jobs' than men, provides grounds from which to refute the binary-based perspective on VOSS. Goldberg (1993) and Baron-Cohen (2003), however, both refer to 'exceptional' women who fall 'outside' normative behaviour according to sex and, to pursue this line of argument, perhaps we might attribute such a description to the 19% of females in the 'male jobs' who tend to be relatively well paid. Yet, turning to the 'mixed jobs' category (49% female), it will be recalled that women follow an extremely similar pattern to that of men in terms of their levels of pay and status. All in all, the women in these two categories ('male jobs' and 'mixed jobs') constitute 49% of the total number of females in the BBC full-time workforce. Hence, it is highly unlikely that they are all 'exceptional' cases.

This type of observation can be applied to those who use Gilligan's 'Different Voice' thesis to explain VOSS. As set out in the previous chapter, this view claims that VOSS is caused by men and women's differing moral perspectives. 'Women's character', purportedly driven by the 'care perspective', is seen to be disadvantageous in the hierarchical workplace, where such traits are valued less than those generated by the male 'justice perspective'. Certainly, many women and men are positioned in stereotypically gendered occupations (as was indicated by the spectrum in Figure 1), with the most female-dominated jobs being, on average, the lowest paid. But, turning again to the women who work within the 'mixed jobs' and 'male jobs' (that is, 49% of all female employees), even a brief inspection of the job titles (for example, radio producer, news presentation and trainer) suggests that such stereotypes are not reflected in reality. If distinctively 'male' and 'female' moral perspectives are as prevalent as the Gilligan view maintains, then why is it that so many women have moved into 'non-female' spheres and are paid well there? Moreover, it is also reasonable to question how an 'inherent moral make-up' is so readily surrendered when faced with a new set of opportunities. For example, while Figure 2 indicates that women are substantially disadvantaged at the top echelons of the organisation, we must take into account that these women are likely to be of a generation from which only around 30% of the female population were educated to undergraduate level. Inevitably, then, there is bound to be a legacy of antecedent disadvantage in contemporary statistics and it should not be assumed that such patterns necessarily reflect a particular set of immutable characteristics.

These results are similarly problematic for proponents of patriarchy theories. If men are consciously set on subordinating their female colleagues, they have not been altogether successful in this context, irrespective of dominant socialising norms and antecedent disadvantages. While there may well be cases of individual sexism or adherence to stereotypes (emphasised in the following chapter), overall, as we have seen, these women at least are able to 'compete' with men quite successfully for the higher paying occupations. This is particularly illustrated by their success in the 'male jobs' and 'mixed jobs'. Inevitably, educational background is likely to be an important cause of the disparity between men and women in the 'extremes' of 'male jobs' and 'female jobs'. This factor appears to be especially significant in the field of engineering, which is featured in many of the job titles in the most male-dominated occupational categories. As reported by the EOC (2005), 85% of engineering and technology undergraduates are male. But this should not be confused with a determined strategy of patriarchy; rather, it is a reflection of trends within education, which, as the EOC further reports, is changing and will no doubt commandeer the occupational choices of future generations.

According to human capital-based theories, VOSS is caused by women's relatively average lower human capital and productivity levels. As we saw in the previous chapter, it is claimed that women invest far more of their 'energy' in the reality or, at the very least, the expectation of their family life duties, thereby limiting their commitment and consequent ambition in the workplace. Hakim (1996) is right to criticise Becker's Rational Choice Theory in denouncing the homogeneity of women as a group; clearly we can see that Becker's theory does not hold in light of these results, as so many women are able to prosper in their careers and command high wages. Although a limitation of these data is that marital and familial status is not recorded, presumably it is not the case that only women in the lowest paid jobs are married with children (as indicated by the following qualitative investigation). If we are to believe the direct correlation between pay and productivity levels, then 49% of the female workforce serve to counter his expectations in the 'male jobs' and 'mixed jobs'. Moreover, we can draw attention to the growing numbers of low-paid 'male jobs' (for example, rigger driver: 94% male with average pay grade of 3.2; or storekeeper: 89% with an average pay grade of 2.2), which indicate a trend unaccounted for by Becker's Rational Choice Theory. A further minor point to note here is the fact that the BBC is an enormously popular employer. Anecdotally it is well known that many people are willing to do jobs for which they are over-skilled and/or over-educated, in order to 'get their foot in the door' of such an organisation. It is worth mentioning this as a reminder of the many reasons people seek particular jobs regardless of their human capital, and it is a crude analysis to assume otherwise, as will be emphasised in the following chapter. All in all, Becker's failure to recognise heterogeneity among women (and among men), irrespective of their marital or parental status, is rightly criticised.

This leads us to Preference Theory, which claims as its raison d'être the circumvention of those particular analytic shortcomings. Admittedly, the results of this chapter might appear rather promising for supporters of Hakim's Preference Theory. The stark pay disparity between women in the lowest paid 'female jobs' and women in the 'male' and 'mixed jobs' would certainly support the view that the so-called 'adaptives' and 'work-centred' women fare differently in the workplace, according to their respective aspirations and preferences. The 'adaptives' (reminiscent of Becker's description of all women), it will be recalled, generally have lower commitment to their employment prospects; consequently, their human capital and productivity levels are much lower than both those of men and the 'work-centred women'. This second group, Hakim suggests, tend to prioritise their commitment to employment, are likely to be childless, and are similar to the men in their preoccupation with higher status careers. Despite numerous counter-claims, it would appear that Preference Theory is too resolute in its description of male homogeneity (as indicated by the variation in men's pay) and it might be suggested that it overlooks the complexity of the male labour force. However, these refutations can be offered satisfactorily only in qualitative terms, which is the purpose of the next chapter.

Notes

[1] For a fuller discussion of segregation measures see Blackburn et al (1999a), Blackburn et al (1999b), Blackburn et al (2001).

[2] As there were very few manual jobs within the BBC occupational groups a comparison with national data is better served by using full-time, non-manual workers.

[3] Journalists and television producers represent the largest numbers of staff in single categories: 2,811 and 1,046 respectively. See Appendix 2 for comparisons with other occupations.

THREE

What people say in the BBC

This chapter explores the themes that underpin the major explanatory theories of VOSS, and scrutinises them through the lens of qualitative analysis. It examines whether the interpretations and attitudes of people, working in an environment infused with substantial levels of VOSS, tally with suppositions intrinsic to patriarchy theories, binary-based theories and human capital-based theories.

Some methodological pointers

The following sections display an abridged version of a large detailed qualitative study (Browne, nd). In order to provide a representative account of a large body of work, detail and head counts have been excluded where possible, and the focus is on emphasising the main emergent themes. These will then be used to test the theoretical explanations of VOSS. The qualitative account of BBC staff views is supplemented with reminders of various theoretical claims, so as to contextualise the sample responses[1].

This part of the research involved interviewing a cross-section of the BBC's full-time labour force about their views on VOSS. Fifty respondents[2] were identified for interview from across five geographical sites in London and Bristol[3]. There were four main criteria for identifying the sample. The first was to locate staff from all pay grades (pay grade 1 to senior management); the second was to ensure that staff from all directorates[4] (or sectors) of the BBC were included; the third was that all respondents were employed on continuous contracts (which increase employment security and career prospects); and the fourth was to obtain a mix of male and female respondents.

Interview topic areas

There were three general areas of discussion: respondents' perceptions of the BBC as an employer; the causes of VOSS; and possible solutions to VOSS.

The BBC as an employer: this topic area was concerned with confirming the BBC as an 'optimal conditions' employer with regard to equality between male and female workers, where the ethos of sex equality was not only strong but also integrated into organisational practices, thereby levelling the playing field between the sexes as much as possible. Locating a competitive environment was also important in order to test the hypothesis that women and men fare differently in the quest to secure the most sought-after jobs. Under such conditions the analysis of comparable men and women (working full time on continuous contracts in a competitive and equality-aware environment) was more likely to uncover the most stubborn root causes of VOSS. The first question concerned the popularity and attractiveness of the BBC as an employer. The second question examined whether the BBC's equality policies are indeed regarded as progressive and successful. The third question aimed to determine whether or not sex discrimination (explicit or latent) was at work in recruitment processes.

The causes of VOSS: this area of discussion emerged as the backbone of the study. Here the aim was to explore the causes of VOSS according to those subject to it, and to analyse the explanations offered against the backdrop of the causal theories previously discussed. Topics discussed included: the biases of senior staff; 'after-hours' culture; male-dominated occupations and departments; preference for male bosses; the masculinisation of female bosses; men and women's career plans; 'career-versus-children-choice'; and sex roles.

Possible solutions: this topic focused on ways in which VOSS might be addressed both in the BBC and wider society. It is the analysis of these research findings in particular that form the basis of the discussion of policy implications in subsequent chapters.

Format of data

For the sake of anonymity, all interviewees are organised into three broad categories of pay grade (in order of seniority). Grades 1-4 are referred to as *basic*; Grades 5-9 (the middle management and specialist category, for example, technical specialists) are referred to as *middle*; and Grades 10-SM1 (the senior management category, which has decision-making authority and generally more autonomy) are referred to as *senior*. Each respondent is numerically coded and in order to contextualise interviewees' perspectives (without disclosing their identities) further details are often included about each person. These are: pay grade category; sex; approximate age category; parental status; education, to at least first degree level; and time spent working for the BBC. For example:

> "These are not really issues that I have given a great deal of thought to before, but now that we are discussing them, I can see how important they are." (No 50: middle, male, 40s, young children, degree, 10 years)

Throughout the following sections such detail is included only where relevant; in many cases respondents are referred to only by code number, pay grade and sex.

During the discussions, many people divulged a great deal of information about their personal lives. These disclosures ranged from petty squabbles with colleagues, or the impact of long daily commutes to work, through to the deaths of loved ones, the failure of marriages, inability to conceive children, or issues surrounding sexuality. It was a tremendous (if unexpected) privilege to have been entrusted with so many personal life accounts. It is not possible to include life histories and specific 'story back-drops' to the responses in this study, but personal elements can be detected in many of the quotations, and these serve to illustrate the parallels and differences between people's circumstances, motivations, aspirations and experiences.

Where the dialogue is self-explanatory no further interpretation is offered. With data of this sort, it would be preferable to give a full range of examples so as to illustrate consensus on certain views despite the heterogeneity of the sample. Naturally, this is not possible here. Hence, unless otherwise stated, it may be assumed that the selected quotations are representative of the views expressed by other comparable respondents.

The BBC as an employer

All respondents confirmed the BBC's popularity as an employer.

> "The thing is, a lot of people try very hard to get into the BBC and are hugely over-qualified and work very hard and really believe in the BBC and so put up with anything, because they know that there is another couple of hundred people waiting for them to leave. I mean, last year's Production Training Scheme had over 3,000 applicants and there were only 15 places!" (No 19: middle, female)

"The BBC has a great workforce because those who are in it are in it because it is the BBC and they want to get on, and so even those in the lowest of grades are massively over-qualified and trying very hard.... We have a very educated workforce and ... everybody who works here actually believes in the corporation – it is not just another product. People come and work for the BBC because they really want to, because they believe in the BBC as a public service which is renowned for its excellence." (No 34: senior, female)

However, the respondents also reported a significant negative aspect to working in such a competitive environment. Some explained how, in their eagerness to get into the BBC, they had been prepared to take much lower paid jobs than they might have been able to secure elsewhere. For example:

"Oh, there are tons of us who are graduates who have just taken anything in the BBC even though our peers outside [of the BBC] are earning loads more – up to three times." (No 14: basic, female)

And, as one very senior manager points out:

"The BBC tries to promote itself to employees by emphasising that the reward factor of working here is not simply the salary. For example, the pension is one of the best in the country, we have good annual leave, and our training is famous. We are very sympathetic with time off and caring issues and so on. We are working continually hard to be a good employer. One of the main problems, of course, is that the government insists that we take up our own financial reins and this affects how much we can raise salaries, and that is to do with the competition against the BBC."[5] (No 30: senior, male)

A similarly positive view emerged regarding the BBC's efforts to secure equal opportunities between its male and female employees[6] by devising extensive and progressive policies:

"Well, the BBC tries very hard to promote equal opportunities for all its staff and applicants and also it tries to provide a service which caters for, and represents, its audience. That's its motivation. That's probably what makes it the best." (No 29: senior, male)

And speaking on the issue of workplace discrimination, we can detect a constant theme:

"My understanding is that, as far as equality goes, the BBC were very much ahead of legislation even 20 years ago; well, more than 20 years ago, because I have been here for 20 years. So I think it has been a very forward looking organisation even in the earlier days." (No 31: senior, female)

Overall (and irrespective of any frustration that may be felt by some), from these examples it would appear that the BBC was seen to offer an attractive environment in which to work, where both men and women were in competition for highly sought-after positions, in circumstances conditioned by a heightened awareness of gender equality and anti-discrimination policy. Especially noteworthy here is the importance of competitiveness and occupational preferences to this particular workforce; these issues will resurface later in the section.

Causes of VOSS

On the causes of VOSS, discussion began with a return to Figure 2 (in Chapter Two), used here to indicate the presence of VOSS. To recap, Figure 2 demonstrates, with striking clarity, the disparity between men and women in terms of pay grades, notwithstanding their similar representation and the respected ethos of equality within the BBC. Following an explanation of Figure 2, each respondent was asked to explain the trend for men to be employed in higher paid occupations.

Managers' biases against women

A pervasive perspective, derived from patriarchy theories, is that VOSS is caused by male strategies designed to thwart women in their attempts to rise through the ranks (see, for example, Bryson, 1992; Valian, 1998).

Indeed, half the respondents (not corresponding to any particular profile) thought that managers' biases were at least one very important causal factor attributable to VOSS. Moreover, there were specific references to sexism. One female television presenter, for example, gave an almost painful account of how she was coerced into transforming herself into something "more feminine for the camera" despite the fact that she – unlike her male co-presenter – was a highly acclaimed expert in her field. The following extract describes something of what she was expected to do when preparing to present a programme on her specialist topic.

> "I would have liked to have thought that the reason for my input was my expertise in this area [subject of programme omitted], but it turns out that it was a case of 'well, your posture is OK, you are going to have to wear a lot of make-up, and you are going to have to change your hair and clothes, but your teeth are all right'. I felt quite strongly that I should be allowed to be myself, but I had to wear high strappy sandals, a padded bra, and do 20 sit ups a day – he [the producer] thought my tummy was too round. And they tried to perm my hair, because he wanted it to have more body. That's when I finally put my foot down.... It is totally different for the male presenters.... My [male] co-presenter was allowed to wear combat shorts and hiking boots, which is what we both should have been wearing [given the terrain]." (No 20: middle, female)

This woman continued her story with an account of how her eventual 'revolt' against this particular producer may have cost her a future contract. Certainly this example might be viewed as a contender for supporting patriarchy theories. Yet in fact this was the only charge of male sexism reported by the sample and, most importantly, it refers to one male individual rather than implying a more general tone of sexism. The following examples demonstrate equally unsavoury accounts of how women are viewed by *female* managers (responsible in both cases for large numbers of basic grade employees).

> "Well, I have to say that all these girlies – sorry – come in as secretaries or whatever and then they are not actually very literate in their jobs, but they spend quite a long time training. And all they want to do is network so that they can get over to Production, and I feel that, to me, is all a waste of time and effort. And I have seen quite a bit of evidence of it here. That doesn't happen with men, funnily enough. All girlie types, all of them [referring to women]. Men seem more direct. They don't go around things like

women. I think that men are better at initiative." (No 25: middle, female)

"Well, I've had a few problems with a particular person within the BBC, making negative references to me for having time off because of the baby.... It was a female manager, who is the same age as me and doesn't have children.... That sort of thing can really be a problem." (No 10: basic, female)

While these examples make reference to latent biases, unfortunately a feature of everyday life, they also, however, draw into question the jump that contemporary patriarchy theories need to make from particular incidences such as these, to the general case of systemic female subordination. The point to be made here is that while various people in senior positions may well have pernicious personal views that seep into their professional life, we should not assume, as patriarchy theories must, a male collective objective to subordinate women. Indeed, the most commonly repeated theme within this context was not the collective male defeat of female colleagues, but rather the negative views of managers (of either sex) regarding maternity leave and childcare.

"Although the BBC is actively encouraging 'equal ops', at the end of the day if you have someone who decides who gets the job and they are thinking about the money side of things, they are not going to sit there and openly say 'this woman may have children'. They are just not going to say that, but I am sure that some think that way.... There is always that suspicion that a woman will put her home life before her job, and that just doesn't happen to men. It isn't very fair. It shouldn't be like that...." (No 7: basic, female)

"I've not come across any cases of discrimination, but I think that women take a lot more time to get to higher levels because men get picked for the top jobs, because overall there is less risk of them leaving, you know, with maternity leave, and it's all about cost. All managers are responsible for their own budgets and that must have an impact on their decisions." (No 8: basic, female)

"Some managers, and they would never admit it, but I'm sure that they still think when they see a female interviewee, 'oh well you are young and you will probably go off and have children at some point. That will cost us extra money and disrupt the departments, working pattern, you know, we will have to pay out for a temp'. So a man is a better bet. I mean, he may leave too, but you know that it won't be because of pregnancy. Do you know what I mean?" (No 18: middle, female)

"I don't think it is a conscious thing, but if you are on a selection board and you are looking for someone ... for long-term commitment, I can imagine that maybe the children issue might come into your judgement. I suppose, if I am honest, as a manager and working within a tight budget, the children issue just might come into it. Whether it is consciously or subconsciously, it could come into it." (No 22: middle, male)

"Certainly managers do think about whether women will go off and have children, there's no question. So what do you do with that?" (No 32: senior, male)

"I have to say that I do understand how men are favoured, particularly in the early 30s age group, because of maternity leave. It is just so disruptive to working patterns, especially in team work." (No 37: senior, female)

'After-hours' culture

In order to investigate the issue of exclusionary patriarchal practices further, respondents were asked whether there was a predominantly male 'after-hours' culture. According to patriarchy theories, this is a realm of informal bonding and exchange of information, which advantages men to the detriment of female colleagues. There were 20 respondents who engaged in 'after-work socialising' on a regular basis, and all 20 expressed the view that the culture had radically transformed and was no longer an androcentric activity.

"It's different now to what it used to be. I think men like it, in a funny sort of way. Things have really changed now that women can go and knock back the beers as good as any man. And you get to find out what is really going on.... And women can be part of that now, I think." (No 8: basic, female, 20s)

"I see no reason why not, I really don't.... Ten years ago there was definitely a problem – it was about who you knew. There is an element of that there still but, as the years go on, it is definitely becoming less important. It has certainly changed. Market forces, to some degree, at most levels have knocked out nepotism and I think that also used to be in men's favour, when the bar was a 'male domain', but not any more really." (No 22: middle, male, 50s)

"There used to be a general consensus that all the jobs and all the deals used to be struck in the bar and so that, in the past, obviously favoured men. But now I don't think that it matters whether you are female or male.... I truly believe that you get the position you go for based upon your merit. 'Who you knew' not 'what you knew' was very much the mechanism for career progression in the BBC and I really think that that has all changed now. If you look at the bar now.... Well, 10 years ago it used to be packed – absolutely heaving – and you knew damn well if you were after a particular job the relevant manager would be there having a 'a few', and your chances were better if you chatted and slipped in your interest. The chances were they would ask you to drop by the office in the morning and 'Bob may be your uncle'! Now, though, they would say 'tough! Ring my secretary for an application form'." (No 17: middle, male, 30s)

"There still is a macho drinking culture especially here in News, but you find a surprising number of women who are just as macho as the men." (No 30: senior, male, 40s)

Many of those who were 'too busy' to socialise with work colleagues (24 in all) were, perhaps unsurprisingly, parents of young children. There were relatively similar numbers of both men and women in this situation[7].

The general ethos appeared to be one of acceptance and inclusion of women, in what has traditionally been seen as an exclusive male domain. As one senior manager put it:

> "In the '70s it was a real 'male thing' – late nights, beer, smoking and lots of discussion about meetings and stuff. It was very exclusionary of women. A lot of the men enjoyed playing the game and tried to keep it as it was. But now things are very different, with women's liberation, and we just don't have that situation now." (No 32: senior, male, 40s)

Of course, these are anecdotal accounts, but still the view that such a culture has largely subsided appears to be standard and poses a considerable challenge to the claim that patriarchal exclusionary practices remain a comprehensive explanation of VOSS.

Male-dominated occupations and departments

The quantitative analysis of VOSS within the BBC produced some clear examples of heavily male-dominated occupations (such as Job 68: technical operator, or Job 74: engineering specialist). Again, it might appear initially that this trend could be explained with reference to theories of patriarchy. To determine whether the evidence confirmed such explanations, respondents were asked if they thought that particular occupations or departments posed specific problems for women's career progression. There were 29 respondents (16 females and 13 males, with no other particular correlations) who thought that, undoubtedly, certain departments were problematic in terms of women's career progression and, what's more, that this was a likely source of VOSS.

> "I think that, particularly in Production, it is heavily biased towards male employees [in terms of career progression] and they tend to move on more because of their specialised qualifications, and most of the women are primarily in the clerical roles." (No 18: middle, female, 30s)

> "Not really in terms of attitude, but maybe in terms of requirements – you know, when people go away on long shooting trips. I think that's harder for women with kids." (No 23: middle, male, 30s, young children)

"Well, as far as the BBC goes, there are some jobs that we can be more flexible with so that the caring issue doesn't have to be such a problem for women. We can make those jobs more family-friendly.... But if you are a correspondent for us and a big story breaks on your patch then you have to go, that's all there is to it, and there's nothing family friendly about that." (No 27: middle, male, 40s, young children)

"I think that here in Production and in News there's a terrible problem in particular. Say now you were working in News, I mean you literally come into the office with your passport in your hand, and that night you don't know whether you are going home or flying off to the other side of world to cover some news story. Now how the hell do you do that if you have young children? I just don't know what the answer is to that." [This respondent is home-based.] (No 36: senior, male, 40s, young children)

"I think that women having kids and that affecting your career does depend on the department you are in. If it is a female-dominated one, then not so much, but in some of the others, then yes. And certainly in Production, with the very long and odd hours, absolutely. It is 'the break', not so much being a woman, that's the problem. I mean, if you took a year or something out, well, a year of technology [missed in a department like Production] – hell fire!" (No 30: senior; male, 40s, young children)

Two distinct features relevant to women's disadvantage in the workplace are revealed by these responses, but neither is attributable to 'patriarchy'. The first is that the requirements of some departments (for example, that workers endure unsociable and long hours, sometimes in geographically distant locations) pose particular problems for those with childcare responsibilities (usually then a default concern for women). The second is that the skewed sex concentrations within particular departments are linked to specific educational backgrounds. A qualification in engineering, for example, was often posited as a prerequisite for many technical jobs and this is still, despite being in a state of transformation, a male-dominated field[8]:

"More women are coming through now with the right educational background and with ... training schemes. We are trying to encourage them onto those schemes, but it will take time for them to climb the career ladder, and we can't just pluck people out and swap them around just for the sake of gender!" (No 35: senior, female, 60s, older children)

In any case, while it is evident that certain types of occupations and departments require commitments that are particularly problematic for those with childcare responsibilities, there were in fact *no* references to 'patriarchy'. One respondent explains:

"I think that it's true that the skills needed for certain jobs are associated with traditional perceptions of gendered approaches. That probably does affect the balance of gender within an organisation, or specific departments within an organisation. But I also think that, to be fair, it is not just the fault of the employer here but also more women apply for supportive secretarial roles, so inevitably there are more women taken on in those roles. What I think this illustrates is that women's perception of themselves is rooted in traditional perspectives and, therefore, that must have an effect as far as segregation goes. Even those who really want to 'make it', for example, those women who want to go up the career ladder in Production, tend to come in as production secretaries doing really menial tasks and here most of them are graduates with a very high standard of degree and some with postgraduate qualifications. It seems crazy! But if these are the jobs they are going for – granted to get their 'foot in the door', but even so – then these are the jobs they are more likely to get." (No 23: middle, male, 30s, young children)

This was a common view among respondents and offers an interesting alternative to the idea that women are in lower status positions within employment hierarchies simply because they are less 'competitive' than men (a view advocated by many from within the binary-based schools of thought); or that women choose lower status jobs because they are less demanding, both in terms of human capital requirements and in terms of commitment and 'energy' (as the human capital-based arguments would have it). Rather, many women may weigh up their chances in what they see as realistic terms. A typical account is given below:

> "I have a degree in Environmental Biology.... When I first came to the BBC, I thought that everyone here would be so brilliant – Einstein – and with years of experience and specialisations. That's why the competition is so high. And so I was delighted and surprised to get a job just as a receptionist.... Now that I'm here, I've realised that not everyone is a genius like I thought but, at the time, I thought I had done really well." (No 4: basic, female, 20s, degree, 11 months)

Many managers' judgements about promotion and recruitment were reported as being based on stereotypes, so it was not surprising to find that many of the women interviewed felt pessimistic about their chances from the outset. But such understandable pessimism is a condition several steps away from either the 'natural predisposition to uncompetitiveness' or the 'laxer commitment' explanations, on which, respectively, exponents of binary-based and human capital-based theories rely.

Preference for male bosses

Interviewees were asked to think about the following view;

> Women (as well as men) prefer to work for male bosses, even when they are not especially competent. Women in positions of authority and power present a serious challenge to sexual identities and sex roles for everyone, not only male colleagues. (Hakim, 1996, p 119)[9]

When asked about this perspective, 33 respondents (18 women and 15 men) either stated 'don't know' or were ambivalent. This is the most significant response and obviously does not tally with the account of an all-round preference for male bosses. Typical examples include:

> "Well, some [bosses] are nice to work for and some are not, it's not a question of which sex they are." (No 2: basic, female, 40s)

"If you really want my opinion, managers are managers because they know how to behave like managers. They are prepared to back-stab, and that's the women and the men – it doesn't matter which." (No 21: middle, female, 40s)

"No, I work with female and male producers [her superiors on various different programmes] and the men I work with at that level are just as likely to burst into tears as the females are! There's no demarcation that I can see. I'm not bothered really." (No 24: middle, female, 40s)

"No, I think it's the type of job you are in that's more a reflection of your personality type [than sex]. I mean, any difference between men and women is negligible in Production because they are all bastards!" (No 29: senior, male, 30s)

"Well, I have worked for some bloody awful women but I didn't have the problem because they were women – it was just because they were bloody awful. I have worked similarly for some bloody awful men, so I don't know. It just depends on the particular person." (No 36: senior, male, 40s)

Only 17 respondents expressed a specific preference regarding the sex of their boss. From these, 10 respondents preferred a male boss and 7 respondents preferred a female boss. Of most interest was the tendency for one sex to prefer the *other* sex as 'boss'. Of the 10 respondents who preferred a male boss, 8 were women; and of the 7 respondents who preferred a female boss, 6 were men. These data hardly conform to the view that, generally, all people have a natural yielding to male dominance, or to the view that men are set on dominating women.

Of the 10 who preferred male bosses, only the two males stated that there were indeed gender differences in personality. They portrayed women as invariably "more moody" and "less organised" than men, and perceived men as "just better at being boss". A more common observation was that female bosses had to be 'harder' than anyone else, often because they were competing for recognition in a male-dominated environment, and this was seen to cause tension in work relations:

"Male [boss]. I am very fortunate. I have to say that I would much rather work for a man because the dynamic of the relationship works better. I think that women are much harder on women. If you work for a woman, it is competitive and they are generally not very forgiving." (No 15: basic, female, 40s)

"I prefer a male boss....Well, there is a tendency for women who are climbing to get to the top that they have to develop a very masculine type of approach, which can be quite difficult to work with as another female." (No 6: basic, female, 30s)

Although these types of responses (which adhere to stereotypical assumptions) may be seen to fit the various theories under review, they remain in the minority as a view. In most cases where respondents expressed preferences for male bosses, those preferences appeared to be based on particular experiences of particular individual managers.

"Male, definitely – I hated working for a woman. She was so hard and aggressive ... she has certainly done well for herself and, in fairness, she probably had a tough time being one of the few women ... but I still hated it." (No 18: middle, female, 30s)

"I think that women are harder when they reach a certain level. I mean, they have to be, and I think that they feel threatened. And I think it is very difficult because they are so isolated among men. My manager has done very well, but she is very domineering and hard ... I would not consider her to be my mentor – she is actually not a very nice person. My old manager was a man, and that was much easier." (No 19: middle, female, 30s)

A considerable amount of discussion emerged around this subject. And, in keeping with the finding that where preferences were expressed they tended to be for the opposite sex (rather than a universal call for male bosses), the following responses elucidate what appears to be a useful skill for work relations.

"Everybody gets what they can, any way they can....They get around things by the 'flirtation technique'. And I think that this is a very effective dynamic between men and women who work together.... Management is a new role for women – they are learning, if you like – and the men are learning to be subordinate. You are not taught to deal with these things in society. Men are still brought up to say 'I will have this done please' and a woman does it. But I think that slowly we will all be forced to learn a middle ground.... There are always teething problems with new ways of doing things." (No 5: basic, male, 20s)

"I think it's just a case of familiarity. I'm a secretary, and most secretaries are women, although we are getting more and more male secretaries, and they are actually seen as a bit of a trophy for the female bosses.... I think men and women like working together. There are certain things that you can achieve, or get away with, with the other sex and that just isn't there with the same sex." (No 14: basic, female, 30s)

"For some men, there is still an assumption and expectation that women are more emotional and, as managers, they are seen to deliberately use emotional reactions and responses to get their way.... And, if I was really honest, I would have to say that does happen sometimes.... I know for sure because I have actually asked ... women about this ... and the response was 'why not? It is another instrument that we can use'. But then that does leave them open to accusations that they are simply emotional creatures." (No 30: senior, male, 40s)

While Hakim acknowledges that the impact of sexuality in workplace relations is important, she interprets this as *exclusive* to acceptance of male dominance:

Male authority is accepted as natural by women, and male bosses are deferred to, even if disliked, because gender and sexuality are central to all workplace power relations, so that a streak of sexual excitement enlivens what is otherwise a master–slave relationship. (Hakim, 1996, p 118)

Certainly we have seen in the previous comments that the notion of natural deferment to male authority is far from consistent. This departure from the stereotype of worker–boss relations is further supported, as we shall see, by the content of discussions regarding personality characteristics of female bosses, often thought to be 'outliers', 'exceptions to the rule', or 'unfeminine'.

Masculinisation of female bosses

Both biological accounts of sex differences pointed towards men's generally greater ability to rise to the top of hierarchies because of their competitive advantage (see Goldberg, 1993; Baron-Cohen, 2003). With this in mind, I asked respondents if they thought women in the higher status jobs were more likely to be seen as peculiar, perhaps unfeminine or in fact masculine in character. Eight responses (4 females and 4 males) were neutral, either stating 'don't know' or were ambivalent. There were 19 respondents who thought that women *were* more likely to be unfeminine/masculine (16 females and 3 males). This question provoked quite a notable split of views between the 'basics' and the other pay grade categories (13 out of these 19 respondents were from the basic pay grade category, and 12 of these were female)[10]. The reasons for this divide are unclear, but it might be suggested that managers at this level are likely to be in constant contact (and conflict) with their subordinates, perhaps prompting more attention and judgement than the superiors of higher grade staff, who tended to be more autonomous. Although the 'basics' were far more likely to think that female bosses were more unfeminine/masculine, the vast majority acknowledged that it was indeed a stereotype.

> "They certainly can do, yes. My boss ... comes across as very hard and a lot of men I know here find her very difficult to talk to.... But I think that it's harder for women to put their point across but not seem aggressive." (No 5: basic, male, 20s)

> "Yes, I think women at that level, they have to play the game. They have to surpass the supposition that they are the weaker sex; they have to over-compensate." (No 18: middle, female, 30s)

> "It's not always the case, but women do appear, when they get to a senior level, to think that you have to change your personality and shout a lot, become dominant.... I'm not saying that all women are bitches – they are not. I know

some extremely nice women, who have always been nice and 'make it' to manager level and have stayed nice. But an awful lot that I have seen have gone from nice women ... into putting this dominating attitude on, which would put anybody's back up.... Puts the male colleagues' backs up and it puts the women below them their backs up too. I don't quite understand why they change." (No 22: middle, male, 50s)

"I do think that women try to base themselves on the image of males in the office, to see how the job should be done or at least the approach that people have been socialised to expect, but I am a bit wary of the generalisation." (No 25: middle, female, 30s)

Coincidentally, one particular very senior female manager interviewed had been referred to previously in this context by another respondent. I asked how she (the manager) had coped being a senior member of a male-dominated department. She responded:

"What I find is that I get accused more of being very loud and aggressive, and I think that's good because most people think that women should be demure and quiet. And I can tell you that if you are demure and quiet you don't get noticed in a room full of men where everyone is yelling and, if you don't yell too, you don't get heard." (No 34: senior, female, 30s)

There were 23 respondents (7 females and 16 males) who did not agree that senior women were more 'masculinised' (only 3 of these are from the 'basic' category). Instead, there were various attempts to phrase answers in terms of the peculiar requirements of managerial procedure rather than in terms of 'masculine' or 'feminine' traits:

"I think it is a difficult subject to broach. The idea itself of masculinity is changing so much that it is difficult to define. If standing up for yourself and acquiring the skills needed to manage a team effectively is masculine behaviour then the answer is 'yes'. But I don't accept that standing up for yourself and being a good manager are masculine behaviours." (No 23: middle, male, 30s)

"I think that the man has to adopt certain ethics, which may not necessarily be natural to him but socially it is accepted as masculine and so easier to pull off. Whereas people tend to be more horrified of women who become hard in the workplace, because it is so different to how we perceive womanhood. You know, in some cases I feel sorry for women in that position. I've really noticed that they are seen as wicked almost." (No 29: senior, male, 30s)

"How can I say that? I judge their personality. They are generally very able and have to train themselves to be very hard. Some are nice, some are not – that's life. Sometimes women who are overly feminine can be just as threatening as someone who is too hard." (No 32: senior, male, 40s)

"You can't make a generalisation about all women and all men. But, I think, because you don't tend to have female bosses so much, it might make a difference to how people see them. What I mean is that they're not the norm. But I'm not sure it's a feminine/masculine thing.... When you are at the senior levels, it is a bit unfair – the labels women get tend to be more negative. It's to do with traditional views rather than the reality." (No 33: senior, male, 30s)

"Organisations are accepting that women are getting into higher positions, so it's becoming more acceptable, but still a lot of people don't see it as the norm. Those [women] who 'make it' are the exception.... They get to the top but they have to be exceptional – more able than the comparative man – and that probably makes them look masculine." (No 32: senior, male, 40s)

"I think that it's less to do with personal characteristics and more to do with the characteristics that you need to adopt in order to cope with what is expected of you in that role, like to be able to sack 500 staff in one go because there isn't enough money to employ them.... I think women are perceived more negatively in that role.... If there are two managers, one a woman and one a man, and they are both getting on with things and sorting things out, the woman will be seen as aggressive and the man will be seen as assertive, which is more positive, I think." (No 34: senior, female, 30s)

All in all, most respondents gave considered accounts of their experiences with bosses, and these did not adhere to male dominance theories. Rather, it was thought that any natural endowments that predispose an individual to becoming a 'good boss' were far more important and relevant than their sex.

Career plans

The quantitative part of this empirical study, set out in the previous chapter, uncovered a stark divide between women in the 'mixed' and 'male' jobs, and those in the lower paid 'female' jobs. At face value, these data would appear to be in line with the tenets of Preference Theory, which claims that there are two general types of working women, the 'adaptives' and the 'work-centred'. The first, who do not actively plan their careers due to the distraction of motherhood (or at least the expectation of it), render their human capital levels far lower than the second group, the 'work-centred'. Conversely, 'work-centred' women are devoted to employment (and likely to be childless, it is claimed), hence are comparable to men in terms of their career progression. It is precisely this divergence of female interest, Preference Theory maintains, that is to the general advantage of men on the career ladder, as their 'profile' is far more mono-functional. Inheriting the legacy of preceding human capital-based theories, Preference Theory argues that the sexual division of labour is a rational maximisation of efficiency, mutually advantageous to those with children. Accordingly, mothers and potential mothers are likely to "accept the sexual division of labour and treat market work as additional, secondary activity, to be fitted in with the demands of domestic life" (Hakim, 1996, p 119).

Although this study is deliberately focused on a full-time workforce within a dynamic 'optimal conditions' and competitive context, there are of course many 'standard' occupations, such as administrative and clerical jobs, for which people may apply without necessarily intending to use them as a spring-board to higher status occupations. These jobs, deemed less stressful and energy consuming, are likely to be those that human capital-based theorists have cited as preferable occupations for the majority of women. Indeed, this perspective was voiced by the following respondent:

"I think women don't wish to go further and this is generic. Take me, for example. I am in my 30s and I now want more of a balance in my life. And even though I have no plans to have a family, I'm not prepared to climb the ladder. I'm not interested in doing that." (No 28: middle, female, married, 30s, degree, 9 months)

However, 23 respondents (14 females, 4 with young children, and 9 males, 4 of whom had young children) intended to pursue progressive career paths and were actively seeking promotion. Although there were no correlations of age, pay grade or length of service, the women were much more likely to have been educated to degree level than the men (15 of these 23 respondents held first degrees – 12 females and 3 males).

"At the BBC, I came in as a PA [personal assistant] to head of [department omitted], which included loads of marketing stuff. Then the BBC decided to become more customer oriented, to keep up with competition, and they set up the [omitted] department and I applied for [a middle pay grade category job – title omitted]. Now, the interesting thing is that I was actually pregnant when I applied for the job, and I got it. I got it in May and went on maternity leave in October.... I think that, personally, too many women think that they cannot manage children and work, and you can, as long as the policy is there to back you up.... I only had secretarial skills when I started, and now the BBC have given me the opportunity to start a Business Masters course.... I really want to make a go of it.... I might not make the DG [director general], but I can have a shot!" (No 10: basic, female, 30s, young children, degree, 2 years)

"Well, I'm extremely competitive.... I intend to go all the way, but I'm not in it just so that I can say 'whooo – I am a radio producer!' I want to actually make stuff that people listen to and learn from. I'm doing a pretty menial job right now, but I am trying very, very hard to break the ranks!" (No 1: basic, female, 20s, degree, 3 years)

"About two months ago, I was offered a position of project manager with another company – a lot more money – but I made the decision to stay in this crap job, because obviously I came here for a reason.... I want to work in Production and perhaps go on to directing documentaries.... And, OK, I'm earning useless money and have no prospects whatsoever at the moment, but you have got to make your own luck, so I decided to stay.... The thing is, I need to work, and I want to progress, but I am very aware now that society labels you by what job you have and it indicates things, like how intelligent you are, etc, so there are so many pressures on you to succeed.... I've got one opportunity in the pipeline. I've been networking and hassling people like crazy.... It's a bit of a long shot, but we'll see what happens in a couple of weeks.... I've been doing work experience for [a BBC production unit – title omitted] during my holidays ... and I'm hoping that will pay off soon." (No 4: basic, female, 20s, degree, 11 months)

This respondent goes on to explain:

"Me personally, I know I want children, so I'm thinking of the future. It's quite murky water though, but the way I look at it is I could be in Production until maybe 35 – you know, really 'dig your heels in' – then have a child, so then I may have to drop out for a bit or whatever. But, at that stage, I will have 10 years' experience behind me in the area I want to be in. I can cross that bridge when I get to it. I will get maternity leave.... I have got to move on – I am climbing the walls now. I was climbing the walls after three months, and the money is terrible. I am not even breaking even at the end of the month at the moment."

"I am on a very junior grade, but not for long – I intend to move quickly. The job doesn't interest me that much, but working for the BBC does. That's why I am prepared to start off so low down. I love the environment." (No 13: basic, male, 30s, degree, 2 months)

"I trained as a teacher, worked as a teacher, then went into the Civil Service.... I have always wanted to work for the BBC, you know, something more creative. So, I did a secretarial course when my girls were a bit older ... came in as a part-time secretary 12 years ago, then I went full time. Then I became an assistant to a producer and then I trained as a producer and I absolutely love my job.... I'm very lucky. Things are looking good for my future prospects." (No 24: middle, female, 40s, older children, degree, 12 years)

From the sample, 10 respondents described themselves, in various ways, as explicitly unambitious (5 females, none of whom had young children, and 5 males, one of whom had young children). No relevant variable correlations presented themselves, apart from the fact that all were from the basic or middle pay grade categories[11].

"No, I don't particularly want to climb to high levels of management. I trained as a secretary because I like it.... The reason I think I got this job was because – unlike the other applicants, so I was told, who incidentally were all women – I was not looking for a 'way in' so that I could cross over to Production. They wanted a serious secretary, who would stay for at least a year and concentrate on the job." (No 5: basic, male, 20s, degree, 6 months)

"I'm not really the ambitious type. I just sort of dropped into this job and I really like it. I don't really have any plans to move on and up to greater things.... I'm not that bothered about career ... I thought working for the BBC would be quite cool ... I mean, you don't wake up one morning when you're four years old and say to your Mum 'I'm going to be a sub-titler', do you?" (No 41: middle, male, 30s, degree, 5 years)

"Well, I was a househusband for three months and I really enjoyed that, and the arrangement really suited my partner. She was really into her career and I could take it or leave it really. I would have continued doing that – I loved looking after our daughter – but I was forced back into the labour market because of money reasons." (No 43: middle, male, 30s, young children, degree, 5 years)

The third set of respondents, 15 in all, was categorised as 'ambivalent' about career making. These people were well trained or educated in their field but, for a variety of reasons, were not actively seeking promotion at the time of interview. Seven were female, 2 of whom had young children, and 8 were males, 7 of whom had young children.

Again, there were no correlations with other variables. Nine of the respondents held first degrees (4 females and 5 males).

> "For me, personally, I really feel that I could have gone on and done a lot more. I have really wasted my education. But, when I got married, that was what was expected then. I had a husband who had a good job, and that was that. And now I look at myself at 45 and a single mum, now that my husband left me and left me to look after the kids. Now I really regret not making more of my career." (No 2: basic, female, 40s, young children, 5 years)

> "I can see myself doing it for two or three years. I went for the job to see what would happen, see whether I would get in, and I got the job. I don't know what I want to do really." (No 9: middle, female, 30s, young children, 13 years)

> "Do I want to try and move into a higher job, do those extra hours in order to impress and work like a maniac to stand out, or do I want to see my child and spend some time with my family? Second option for me, please! Now, if that means that a career opportunity comes up for me in the next 12 months that I should go for, I am actually not going to go for it, although I have been advised to. So I expect it is even harder for women in the same context. So, no wonder there is this trend [pointing to Figure 2]." (No 27: middle, male, 40s, young children, degree, 13 years)

> "I came here straight from school and now I'm kind of doing OK. I've been here all my working life and I've moved around a lot, sometimes upwards, sometimes sideways. I'll just stick around for another 15 years and see what happens." (No 40: middle, male, 30s, young children, 10 years)

The main point to focus on here is the diversity of career projections, irrespective of sex and parental status. Of particular note is that a lack of career strategy and ambition is not exclusive to women. Here we see that there are also men who could be termed Preference Theory 'drifters', despite being in a competitive and hierarchical employment structure. Ironically, those men who were categorised as 'not ambitious' were far more likely to have young children than the females. Thus, the extent of diversity within, as well as across, the sexes generates a considerable challenge to claims of human capital-based theories, binary-based theories or indeed those founded on theories of patriarchy. According to these same perspectives, women follow lower status careers paths and occupations either by virtue of rational choice because they are 'less competitive', or as a result of patriarchal forces. This topic was the focus of the next discussion.

Career or children?

I asked respondents if women had to make a choice between preferred careers and motherhood.

Only 5 respondents from the sample (4 females and 1 male, all in their 30s and 40s, 2 of whom had young children) thought that women's career choices were not limited by motherhood, and their comments suggested that they thought policy provisions comprehensively catered to the needs of working mothers[12].

> "No, not so much now – maybe 10 to 20 years ago. Women try to juggle more now than they tried to do in the past and, with all the policies, it's much easier to hang on in there." (No 2: basic, female, 40s, young children)

> "I can absolutely promise you that women are not forced to make that choice. It used to be definitely the case years ago, but not now. We have put a great deal of effort into developing policies which enable women to manage both children and their work life so that they can do both if they wish to." (No 30: senior, male, 40s, young children)

There were 11 respondents (8 females and 3 males) who thought that women did indeed have to choose between career and motherhood. The general view among these respondents was that motherhood had a negative impact on work patterns and increased the task load of surrounding colleagues. (All respondents related these issues to data in Figure 2.)

> "Yes, and I think women with children should make a choice. If I am working in an office with someone with two young children, and they get a 'phone call and say 'can you come and collect the kids straight away and take them home because they have chickenpox', and that is two weeks

out of that month, and you are left picking up all the pieces, thinking 'hold on, this just isn't fair – we are all being paid the same money for the same job'.... Generally, I think that it is important to help people who need it, but I think somehow the line has to be drawn, because those people who don't have those extra commitments will be left covering for the others who have." (No 6: basic, female, 30s)

"This might sound quite hard, and I am speaking as a married women, but a married woman without children. Women colleagues who have children and try to have a career full time – and I understand when women say 'no I have to go I have to pick up the kids or whatever'; fair enough, I understand that. But, at the same time, someone like me would then have to cover a bit, and then is it fair that someone like me who is married, you know has a family but without kids, so they say 'oh well you can do it', and I think 'well, I might not have children but I have other commitments', and I don't think that's fair. I think women with children should be made more aware of this, and consider the impact that it has on the rest of us." (No 15: basic, female, 40s)

The majority of respondents, however, thought that effectively women were forced to make an unfortunate choice between having children and pursuing a career, and they saw this as a root cause of VOSS (making reference to Figure 2).

"I think that it is certainly true of a lot of women.... I think that there is a fear that, if you take time out ... then you will be pushed back down to the bottom of the pile of potential people who are all trying to scramble their way to the top." (No 6: basic, female, 30s)

"If you want to take a break to have the children then you can do – that's not the problem. What holds women back is that, when you have the main role of looking after a child, then you have to think about what job you have, because you cannot be working God knows how many hours, because the child is your responsibility.... That is why it is easier for men and the jobs that they are doing, because they can do the longer hours, which usually puts them in a better position for promotion, etc." (No 9; middle, female, 30s, young children)

"Well, yes. I am vaguely uncomfortable saying this, but I think that the gender difference [referring to Figure 2] is to do with domestic and personal commitments. I think that when you get to around Grade 5, to Grade 7 ... it starts to become increasingly difficult for people with childrearing responsibilities. The demands get tougher and women are always left holding the baby, as it were." (No 23: middle, male, 30s, young children)

"Yes, I think that it does happen, but it's not as simple as choosing or not choosing between children and career. I think women are sometimes scared to take the time off to have children because it brings you out of the work cycle.... I am 36, and I can tell you that the reason why I have left it so late to have children is because of my career. And getting pregnant was an accident – a happy accident – but if it had not happened, I really feel that I would not have been able to make a decision to have one, because of the pressure of my career.... It is hard, and sometimes I think about the fact that I probably won't have any more, and I would like to." (No 19: middle, female, 30s, young children)

"I don't think that it is a lack of trying or ability on the women's part. I know a lot of women who would happily like to climb the career ladder and are extremely able. I think you know that in society as a whole, and not just in the BBC ... there are a lot of very able women who, because they have kids, perhaps are not able to fulfil their potential. Society needs to go a long way before we can sort that problem out." (No 29: senior, male, 30s)

These views appear to be rather at odds with the principle that women's employment status is a consequence of their *preferences*, as human capital theories, in particular Preference Theory, would have us believe. Rather, what we are hearing loud and clear here is a widely held conviction that women's actual choices are more often than not a consequence of limited available options when it comes to genuinely combining parenthood and career. Even though the 'division of labour' is *common* between men and women, it is not safe to assume that it is, as both Hakim and Becker believe, attractive to all those who experience it.

Diminishing traditional sex roles

Underpinning human capital-based interpretations of VOSS is a binary-based explanation of the motivation for sex-role specialisation. It is claimed that sex-related predispositions determine role specialisation. On this subject, respondents were asked if they thought that traditional sex roles were diminishing. The majority of respondents (41 in total, 22 females and 19 males) thought they definitely were[13]. All but one saw the conflation of sex roles not only as a positive shift in attitudes, but also welcomed the increase in men's involvement in the practical duties of parenting:

> "Oh yes, things are really changing now. But when I had mine [children], I had to give up my job and stay at home, then go back again later, so there was no career path for me…. But things are very different now for the younger ones. The men are getting more involved in the home and it's taking a lot of the pressure off the women." (No 3: basic, female, 50s)

> "Yes, I think today that a lot of relationships are more 50/50. I don't think that if a child is sick, for example, that the woman is automatically the one to go home and deal with it any more." (No 7: basic, female, 20s)

> "Yes, I think so, definitely. Men are much more involved in their families. If I look at the difference between the way my father was with us and the way my brother is now with his kids…. Oh yes, definitely." (No 12: basic, female, 20s)

> "Oh yes, I do think that men are getting more and more involved in the childcare role, and I can see that progressively making a difference to women's experience of work in the future." (No 29: senior, male, 30s)

> "I've really noticed that it's not just the women who don't want to work ridiculous hours. I think things have really changed. Men seem to be much more involved with their kids than they used to be." (No 35: senior, female, 60s)

"When I did my research here, I found that the key things that came out were that people needed more flexibility because of childcare. Don't get me wrong, the BBC is very conscious of these issues, but things seem to be changing in general. It wasn't just the women who were pushing for more flexibility – and I find this really interesting – it was a lot of men, who wanted exactly the same thing, but they were saying that they didn't feel like they could always come forward and say it." (No 31: senior, female, 40s, young children)

Of particular interest (as implied by that last quote), were examples of traditional sex role *reversal*:

"I earn more than my husband and I think he would become a househusband if it really came down to the nitty gritty. He is good – he drops the baby off every morning and picks him up in the evenings. I don't, because he works a bit closer to where the child-minder is." (No 10: basic, female, 30s, young children)

"It's funny actually, because the guy I work with and his girlfriend are just about to have a baby and she earns a lot more than him. So, anyway, she is going to go back to work and he is prepared to do the domestic bit. So, yes, things are definitely changing, it's great. The focus is on what works for you." (No 17: middle, male, 30s)

"I accept that it is very tough for women. But also, as people always seem to forget, I, as a man, have had no alternative but to slog through working for my entire life. I would have loved to have had a year or two off, not working.... When I say 'off', I know that childcare is very hard work, you know what I mean – a couple of years different with my kids. So both women and men with children are disadvantaged, that's what I think. Mind you, more and more men are saying that they also have families and would like to go home at a reasonable hour now. That's definitely changed ... I mean, I know of three families where the man stays at home and the woman earns the money, whereas five to 10 years ago I would not have known any. I know that's not a lot, but I think it is a significant move towards that way of doing things." (No 36: senior, male, 40s, young children)

It is worth remembering here how Preference Theory and, more generally, the binary-based theories, resist the notion of such sex role reversal:

> Even career women refuse to marry and maintain househusbands: women who earn enough to be breadwinners themselves, who can afford to keep a non-earning or low-paid husband, and who constantly bemoan the fact that most men have the support services of a wife at home whereas they do not, even these women refuse to contemplate role reversal and become economic supporters rather than joint earners in a dual-career household.... Goldberg is right to underline this *joint* refusal of men and women to contemplate role reversal at home as telling us something important about relations between the sexes. (Hakim, 1996, p 204; emphasis in the original)

However, somewhat surprisingly, among this sample of 50 people there were three women who had 'househusbands' and one man who had previously been a househusband (see respondent No 43 in the previous discussion on 'Career plans'). Here are some examples:

> "I am the breadwinner in our family and my husband looks after our son. It was not a conscious decision – my husband lost his job. But I can see that he is much happier now than he ever was before when he worked long hours in the City.... There is no way I could have continued with my career if I had to do all the domestic and childcare stuff too ... in fact, I have taken on more work responsibilities since I have had [name of child omitted], but I know that I have had to compromise being with him. But then my husband does it instead. Nothing is ideal, but this works better for us." (No 19: middle, female, 30s, young children)

> "I think things are really changing. Many men think more about the quality of life and don't want to do the long hours any more, and this has made it easier for women to do work in higher grade areas.... My husband is actually a 'home husband' ... he is the one who looks after our little

baby girl. He doesn't earn as much as me, and also he doesn't have a permanent contract. He works in [BBC department omitted], but on the technical side and can work from home or on sporadic contracts. Also, when our daughter was born we decided that, between us, we didn't want to lose her 'growing up' period to child carers.... Also, in this way, we save the £600 per month that we would have had to spend on childcare. I notice that when I get in, the shopping is done and a meal is cooked and I think to myself 'God, no wonder men have had it easy for so long', because it is a weight off your mind to have that kind of support. I think that this tells us a lot about gender roles and advantages." (No 31: senior, female, 40s, young children)

"Well, I would have to say that things can change.... My husband was made redundant a few years ago and now he stays at home with our children. So, to be honest, it wasn't planned to do things that way ... but I earn a good salary and like my job here very much, so it just made sense. He probably wouldn't have chosen to do it had things been different at the time, but now he says that he is a much happier person ... he used to have an incredibly stressful job and was always away a lot with work, but now he has taken up [occupation omitted], which he can fit around the kids ... so it's completely different to the job he had before, but he is a different man. I don't think that he would change it now, and the kids love it." (No 38: senior, female, 40s, young children)

We have seen here that it is a mistake to assume men and women necessarily conform to 'naturally' determined stereotypical masculine and feminine roles. This observation categorically challenges the claims of the binary-based theories and human capital-based theories, which rely on notions of male dominance, role specialisation and the idea that women are invariably coerced into particular roles by men – a tenet of patriarchy theories.

Possible solutions to VOSS

Having collected the various views on why VOSS persists in the BBC (an 'optimal conditions environment'), respondents were asked to consider the discussion thus far and to comment on whether they thought anything could be done to alleviate the disparity between men and women in terms of pay and status.

The responses varied considerably. Thirteen respondents (6 females and 7 males) stated that they did not know (no particular characteristics correlated). Five respondents, all females without children, stated that they couldn't see how things would get any better. Two respondents, both from senior grades, thought that women's representation in the higher grade occupations would improve with time, as younger generations with more egalitarian attitudes filtered through. Traditional attitudes towards sex roles, they thought, were a crucial factor in explaining VOSS.

The remainder of respondents, however, focused on policy reform as the necessary response to VOSS. (There were 32 in total; 16 females, including 5 with young children, and 16 males, 9 with young children.) The issue of crèche facilities was a common theme among this group. Although many praised the BBC for in-house childcare provision, there were several comments about the lack of places actually available. For the collective London sites there were only 65 crèche places, and for the Bristol site there were only 30.

> "If we could provide more good nursery care then we could get more work for women. I know that there is an enormous waiting list. We just managed to get one of our staff in whose husband died, but that's what it took to get a place – the baby is three months old. It is good to have provision ... I think with having the nursery you get a better approach from the women. The woman I work with upstairs has just had a baby and has to put him on the list now to get just two mornings a week care in a year's time, so that's another reason why a lot of women are simply not able to concentrate on their careers or come back to work even." (No 34: senior, female, 30s)

Many thought that those who were seen to be more 'valuable' staff would be more likely to acquire crèche places:

> "What I think is bad is that the higher status people get the majority of the crèche places, and there are only a few places, and they are the ones who can actually afford to pay for private care. But I guess they're deemed as more 'precious', so it's hard luck on the lower grade women." (No 15: basic, female, 40s)

"Well, I was quite shocked when I learned how we actually pick those who get the most crèche places. Did you know that it really depends on how valuable that person is to the BBC, and who their boss is, and what kind of pressure they administer?" (No 25: middle, female, 30s)

"[Department x] has the majority of the crèche places here. Resources, for example, only has a couple of places. Who you work for is crucial here... [Department x] produces the big money here, so it gets the [crèche] places." (No 12: basic, female, 20s)

Affordability of crèche places was a fundamental stumbling block for many employees with dependent children:

"There are lots of people here who, despite the fact that it [the nursery] is subsidised, still would not be in a position to afford it. I'm one – I just could not afford to spend an extra £100 a week, and what if you had two or more children?" (No 6: basic, female, 30s)

"I am one of the really lucky ones. I have a little boy in the nursery [the cost of which is £100 per week]. The nursery is 9am to 6pm and, well, I can't get that anywhere else; most nurseries close at 4 [pm]. I rarely leave the office until 5.55 [pm], so they get a free extra hour out of me for that. But still the major problem is the expense. I think it should be subsidised more. I have to say that I really struggle to pay for it and, well, if I had another child to consider I just couldn't stay working." (No 19: middle, female, 30s, young children)

For many, unpaid leave offered under the EU Parental Leave Directive (details of which are discussed in the following chapter) was an unworkable solution to childcare dilemmas.

"I mean, you would have to think twice about taking unpaid leave. I just couldn't afford to, and I am sure I speak for most people, so what's the point of it?" (No 9: middle, female, 30s, young children)

"I think that parental leave has the potential to impact on 'the old ways'. I think it could change it all. I would take it definitely. The problem with the policy is the pay issue. The only people who could afford to use the [EU] directive at the moment are those who didn't need it in the first place. The money makes all the difference, so it's just rubbish. I think that it has to be backed up financially in order to make a level playing field. And, in that case, a lot of men I know would definitely do it. Three months is not very long at all in career terms [this respondent was a househusband for 3 months], but *crucial* in developing a relationship with your child. There's just not justification for not doing it really, and it made all the difference to my partner. She could carry on [with her career] when it was a crucial time for her." (No 43: middle, male, 30s, young children)

"Personally, if we could afford it, I would love to take a couple of months' parental leave and look after my kids while they are still really young. But until it provides some financial support then we just can't afford to do it." (No 42: middle, male, 30s, young children)

"A lot of people are interested in the [EU Parental Leave] directive but, the question is, can they afford to take it off? Not many can. I think paid parental leave would make a hell of a difference. I would; well, I wouldn't have an option, my wife would make me! The more flexibility you have, the better equipped you are to get equal conditions for people. You have to give them more of a chance to organise themselves accordingly to what suits them best. Mixed [women and men] and funded caring provision will help those that want it." (No 46: middle, male, 30s, young children)

"If you think about it, everyone here, even those at the very top, we were all children once. Children grow up and then they have their own children, and so on. We all know that, and there is such a separation between that part of life and the other crucial part – work. Why the hell organisations don't recognise that and organise themselves around *that* rather than the other way round, you know? As a [title omitted] manager of the BBC, what am I doing about changing things and letting my voice be heard? Not a lot really! The thing is, employees accept that the organisation has never, and will never, organise itself around people's lifestyles. They accept that deal. What else can they do?" (No 27: middle, male, 40s, young children)

Most respondents referred to practical measures as a possible solution to (or at least alleviation of) what they saw as the main causes of VOSS, namely issues surrounding childcare. Crucially, several respondents drew a distinction between mothers with different levels of income:

> "A lot of the senior women here absolutely depend on their nannies if they have kids, and that makes a big difference in how far they can go with their career, and obviously most cannot afford it. Probably the women at the top here are much older too. They have had their kids and have been back for years, probably; no good for the younger ones, though!" (No 15: basic, female, 40s)

> "The women in the more senior bands are in that 45-50 age bracket, but the reason that there are less [than men] is because there are less women that manage not to have let children slow them down career-wise. They're the type that have got money and can afford help, and that makes a *huge* difference." (No 17: middle, male, 30s)

> "If you earn big bucks, you can afford a nanny, etc. You have a choice. But for most that is *not* an option." (No 14: basic, female, 30s)

That there are *practical* advantages to being a highly paid senior female employee with children, compared to being a lower paid mother, indicates clearly that extending subsidised provision is an obvious way to achieve better balance between childcare and work demands for women. It also counters claims that mothers necessarily *prefer* less demanding and consequently lower occupational status than men, as outlined by human capital-based theories.

The last discussion topic concerned the level of people's actual support for further provision of services and benefits. At the beginning of the interview, respondents were asked what they thought was the meaning of 'equal opportunities policy' (specifically related to men and women). All responded similarly, essentially stating that everyone should be given the same opportunities in the workplace, irrespective of sex:

> "Regardless of sex, that you could get to any position within the BBC you wished to; to make sure you all get treated the same, with the same opportunities available." (No 2: basic, female)

> "That people are treated the same, regardless of sex, so that there are no differentiations which they experience in terms of firstly joining the BBC, and then to participate and develop within the organisation." (No 26: middle, female)

> "I understand it to be that you would move any barriers that are perceived in order that everyone can meet their full potential." (No 31; senior, female)

> "To try to make sure that we reflect the nation that we broadcast to, in terms of the people we employ.... So, as an employer, it's all about diversity; making sure we give the same chances to people with very different backgrounds, and the sex of the individual is all included in that way of thinking." (No 36; senior, male)

However, it has already been shown that the majority of respondents viewed childcare duties and career progression as uncomfortable bedfellows under current policy arrangements, and that such an ill fit certainly led to VOSS. Bearing in mind the common definition of 'equal opportunity policy' and the universal support it receives, it may be thought that increased provision (whether it be more crèche facilities or payment of benefits during parental leave, for example) would be seen as an obvious contribution to creating a more accommodating environment for those who have children. Yet, when asked if respondents would support increased provision, the responses were far from unanimous.

The following responses refer to the increase of provisions in general. Several different issues are mentioned, although the main focus of analysis is to assess the amount of support for extended benefits.

Five respondents were ambivalent (4 females, none of whom had children and 1 male who had young children):

"It's all about money, at the end of the day. If you have children it does cost you more, or ageing parents. If you are single, gay, or childless, etc, you have more income so you should not be disgruntled at benefits for those who need them to work effectively. On the other hand, I think it is crazy. If you are not careful you will end up providing so much for people, which costs the taxpayer more money. There has to be a balance. I just don't think that the employer should have that kind of responsibility. I think that you have to look at a job advert and decide whether you are in a position to do it or not." (No 25: middle, female, 30s)

"It is very difficult to say. The BBC stands up very well in comparison to other companies as far as policies go. But what has been on the increase in the past few years is that people approach line-managers with equal opportunity issues of any kind. The first question the line-managers ask is 'how much is it going to cost?' And if the cost is too high, then it will be 'well I'm sorry if the cost is too high, I can't do it'. I'm sympathetic ... if it is paid for corporately (whatever the hell that means, but basically if the BBC is going to pay for that then I am right behind you), but if it has to come out of my budget then it is going to be much more difficult." (No 36: senior, male, 40s, young children)

Seven respondents (5 females, 1 with young children, and 2 males) stated that they would not support further financial and childcare facilities. There was no age correlation, but all respondents were from either the basic pay grade category (4 respondents) or the middle pay grade category (3 respondents).

"I think that I would resent it now, because I never had any help with my children. Effectively, you are making their salary higher. Then you should give everyone a rise. It would cause unrest between the workforce – everyone would get fed up." (No 3: basic, female, 50s, older children)

"I think the whole idea is totally out of order. I am a working mum, but I do not expect any perks from the BBC whatsoever." (No 9: middle, female, 30s, young children)

"Well, I guess it is like what is happening now. I am young, fit, healthy and single – I have no dependants – and yet I am paying for kids to be educated or kids imprisoned. I wouldn't want to support any more projects like that one too much, because then it may be that the wages in the company would suffer." (No 11: basic, female, 40s)

"I would resent it. I don't think that you should be provided with perks just because of your private life choices. My boss waltzed in with a new child and wanted to work four days a week. Well, that was no good. And if she only wants to work four days a week, why should she get on? It doesn't seem fair. *I* would like to work four days a week." (No 18: middle, female, 30s)

"Well, if I had young children then I might take advantage of the crèche, but I don't really see I should expect that there should be a crèche place for me, or why the BBC should have to pay for people to be able to go to work. I regard it as my responsibility to organise childcare." (No 21: middle, female, 40s, older children)

In contrast, 36 respondents (17 females and 19 males) replied with enthusiasm at the prospect of more benefits (sometimes even when they anticipated that such provisions might affect their own wages, although this was not stipulated in the questioning). All but 2 of the respondents with young children were included in this category.

"I feel that one day I want to take advantage of that, so I am naturally in favour. I can't imagine how I would feel being on the other end, knowing that I am never going to take advantage of those kinds of benefits, but I don't think that I would not want it to be there for other people, especially if it were to cover caring across the board and not just children. Wouldn't you like to think that you were human enough to support a system like that, because there were other people who really needed it?" (No 7: basic, female, 20s)

"I think a negative attitude towards provision systems is a bit childish: 'you've got, I must have'. I mean, people's circumstances change through life, and certain people get certain advantages at certain times. It all pans out." (No 22: middle, male, 50s)

"And I am sorry, but any person who whinges about wanting extra perks to balance it all out is a person talking about financial issues for themselves, not equality. No, I would not be bothered. We want people to be able to work, so you have to provide the basics for them, and I consider childcare a basic." (No 33: senior, male, 30s, young children)

"Flexibility is the main thing – letting people make choices on how best they can cope with all the aspects of their life, while ensuring that they can get the job done, whether that be paid leave for men, or more childcare facilities.... Of course, there will always be some resentment but there shouldn't be. Let me put it this way: if you don't have a car, you shouldn't moan about not having a parking space!" (No 45: senior, male, 40s, young children)

"I think if parental leave were paid it would really take the wind out of the sails of bigots. It would definitely work to diminish stereotypes, say in 20 years.... I think it's a really good idea." (No 48: middle, male, 20s)

"Well, kids are necessary in the great scheme of things, so perhaps the question should be turned around: you choose for whatever reasons not to have kids, so you don't get paid leave for them. That's that!" (No 42: middle, male, 30s, young children)

It is abundantly clear from these interviews that childcare provision is key in addressing VOSS, but that to expect the employing organisation to manage to provide sufficient provision is unworkable. As one senior male explained:

"My opinion is that organisations are not very good at managing nursery facilities. I wouldn't bring a three year old into the centre of London at 6.30 in the morning, it's just not viable." (No 32: senior, male, 40s, young children)

Clearly a broader approach is necessary, and shared state/employer-subsidised childcare in local settings is one obvious proposal. The majority of respondents (regardless of parental status) thought that a more even-handed, universal approach to provision for (primarily) childcare was vital. The second key observation was the lack of practical options open to men who wished to improve their parent/work balance. This lack of options was not only deemed unfair and impractical by respondents, but was also a source of the role demarcation that is clearly at the root of VOSS.

Implications

The claims to explain VOSS posited by the various causal theories under analysis can now be analysed in relation to these qualitative data.

Theories of patriarchy

In short, the evidence simply did not surface in support of these theories. Men were not charged with collectively organising themselves in the communal quest to subordinate their female colleagues. This is not to deny, of course, individual cases of misogyny or sexism. There was clear evidence of discriminatory attitudes towards women; however (and crucially), those who held such views were managers of *either* sex, not simply men. This is a vital distinction, which pulls motivational explanations away from patriarchal forces and towards the practical concern that demands of childcare (most often deemed to be exclusively those of women) are highly disruptive to working patterns – an assumption clearly correlated with VOSS.

It was not the case that women were still largely excluded from the bastions of career-boosting social engagements after work (in so far as they still exist), nor that the existence of male-dominated departments was illustrative of exclusionary domains consisting of the 'best jobs', which, as we saw from the quantitative data, are more likely to be in mixed-sex sectors. Instead, we have seen evidence of shifts in social attitudes towards women as agents in the public sphere. Counter to the logic of this causal perspective, we can expect that appropriately skilled women will gravitate towards the better-paid jobs so long as practical conditions permit. As horizontal trends in education start to spread (and aided by these very attitudinal changes), there seems no reason to suppose that in future patriarchal forces will spoil the progress of women in non-traditional female sectors of the labour force. The lack of childcare provision and economic restrictions are much more likely candidates than patriarchy to explain 'career paralysis'. In a contemporary context such as this study, patriarchal theories are moribund as comprehensive analytic tools of VOSS.

Binary-based theories

The claim that women naturally concede to male domination was far from evident. The majority of respondents were not concerned about the sex of their boss but, rather, with individual personalities. For the minority who did have a preference, it was shown that they tended to prefer the *opposite* sex. Another counter-example to this type of explanation for VOSS was the dominant view regarding the character of female bosses. When asked if women in higher status jobs were more masculine in character, the majority thought not. Even for those who thought that senior women acted in an unfeminine way, this was largely understood as an act of 'compensation' for being among high-flyers at a senior level. This form of 'exaggeration' of 'male traits' was not, however, seen to be an indication of 'unnatural' women on the fringes of female personae, but simply an adopted coping strategy.

A further illustration of how the heterogeneity of preferences cuts across sex was shown by the fact that men were as likely as women to vary in their career ambitions. While women are more likely to take employment breaks due to childbearing, this was not shown necessarily to impact on women's career progression, in comparison to non-mothers, provided they returned to work within the standard terms of maternity leave. The very fact that many men were not seen as necessarily more motivated to progress weakens the claims of the binary-based theories. Indeed, more generally, the argument that men will inevitably predominate in any hierarchy was not borne out within this sample, not least with reference to those men who, when they did assert a preference for the sex of their boss, preferred a female. On a similar topic, the majority of respondents stated that traditional sex roles were diminishing, and this appears to be consistent with the common call to develop mechanisms through which work and childcare can be balanced more equally between the sexes. Overall, then, we can see that the results we expect according to the binary-based theories were lacking. Instead, we find a move towards individual interest manifest in numerous preferences, which do not necessarily align themselves with the supposed gender traits that the binary-based theories claim.

Human capital-based theories

Lastly we turn to the human capital-based theories, namely Rational Choice Theory and Preference Theory. As discussed previously, these theories are largely dependent on the inevitability of sex-role specialisation. Again, these data did not reflect the characteristics posited by such theories. The diversity of 'career plans' among both men and women showed no significant pattern of 'male solidarity', the notion on which the human capital-based theories rely to explain the motivation for men and women to adhere to sex-role specialisation. This point in particular serves to contest Preference Theory, which supposes that women are divided in their career outlook while men predominantly are not. Moreover, the respondents' preferences in terms of realistic career plans (indicative of their commitment to career/ employment) were not reflected by their current pay levels, apart from the fact that none of the senior pay grade respondents was classified as 'not ambitious', which is perhaps to be expected. These findings fly in the face of both Preference Theory and Rational Choice Theory.

Comments

Although the aim of this part of the research has been to raise live issues as people see them, not only in the BBC but also in society more generally, it is instructive (despite the small numbers of the sample) to note the individual respondents' particular arrangements for coping with the demands of work and parenting. Of the 6 women with very young children, 3 were dependent on househusbands. As for the others, one woman shared childcare duties equally with her husband and, while they were both at work, she used a registered child-carer (who happened to be a close friend and who charged much less than the market rate). One depended on her family for childcare after school hours, and the other relied on the BBC crèche. The important point here is that these kinds of childcare arrangements are not likely to be readily available to women at a national level. Hence, although it may be argued that these various ways of combining one's family and employment represent a 'rational choice', it cannot be assumed that sex-role specialisation is inevitable or even practicable in this environment – a progressive environment, nonetheless.

These are crude measures but they are nevertheless indicative of the fact that there is more to human capital and productivity levels than one's sex and parental status. As Burchell and Rubery have forcefully argued:

> If one accepts that observed labour market phenomena are the outcome of complex interactions between a large number of institutions (eg employers, the education and legal systems, the family, etc), it becomes difficult to justify any analysis that attempts to establish simple causal pathways. (Burchell and Rubery, 1990, p 565)

Many respondents felt that to take child-related leave (particularly if for a relatively lengthy period or on several occasions) might have adverse effects on human capital levels, although this was particularly expressed as a problem in the highly technical areas of the BBC. While leave from employment does not inevitably result in subsequent lower human capital or productivity levels, it is worth considering how many respondents experienced difficulty in combining childcare and employment, a problem that effects most mothers to varying degrees. To assume that the motive for strict sex-role specialisation is a 'natural' predisposition, as the binary-based and human capital-based theories suggest, is clearly unfounded. Rather, it seems much more likely that structural constraints and sex stereotypes are a direct cause of the restrictions that many parents face in the labour market.

The majority of respondents held the view, directly related to this issue, that traditional sex roles were on the decrease. Moreover, there were several cases of, and references to, role-reversal within this sample. Contrary to the arguments of the human capital-based theories, it is not inevitable that 'sex-role specialisation' is either attractive or necessarily 'mutually advantageous' to men and women, particularly as it was seen that in many cases men were (or at least wanted to be) more involved with the day-to-day upbringing of their children. Given the current array of practical options available, most of the sample did not feel that the choice made by some women between childcare and employment was always a question of 'preference', but often of necessity – an unfortunate predicament. The majority of respondents pointed to, and supported, the improvement and expansion of provision for *both* men and women as parents, as a possible solution to the limitations of women's career progression and as a way of extending the possibility for men to play a more active role in raising their children.

The next chapter will show how current policy provisions, although designed to create equality between men and women, ironically serve to 'herd' individuals into stereotyped positions that do not necessarily bear any relation to their actual preferences.

Notes

[1] A detailed account of methodological approaches and justifications, the full content of the interview aide-mémoire, and a much fuller empirical analysis of these data are found in Browne (nd).

[2] The numbers of respondents by sex and pay grade are as follows: within the basic grade, there were 4 males and 12 females. Within the middle grade, there were 13 males and 9 females. Within the senior grade, there were 6 males and 6 females. By ensuring that all criteria were accounted for in the sample, it was not possible to secure equal representation of each criterion across the sample. For example, overall there are 27 females and 23 males as opposed to 25 of each. These discrepancies should be noted when comparing responses, although the purpose of this exercise was not to quantify the exact number of responses by each criterion, but rather to gain a general idea of people's views on the salient issues surrounding VOSS from a cross-section of the workforce. Half (24) of the sample have children, 18 (6 females and 12 males) of those 24 have young children, and 31 (18 females and 13 males) are educated to degree level. See Browne (nd) for further breakdowns.

[3] Although I was inundated with replies to my request for interviewees from many of the numerous BBC sites (137 in the UK alone), I chose to concentrate on just five sites for obvious logistical reasons. The four London sites were: Broadcasting House (799 total number of staff); Langham Street (149); Television Centre (5,874); and White City (1,984). In Bristol the location was Broadcasting House, which employs a total of 828 staff.

[4] The various sectors of the BBC under analysis are divided into 'directorates'. The number of respondents from each is as follows: central directorate: 10; production directorate: 11; resources directorate: 10; news directorate: 8; broadcast directorate: 11.

[5] However, it should be noted that the BBC does not pay disproportionately low wages compared to the national average.

[6] Although respondents were asked specifically whether men and women enjoyed equal opportunities, some interviewees mentioned other equality-related issues. Older respondents and a disabled respondent praised the BBC for its attitudes towards age and disability. For example, one interviewee (senior, female) stated that "the attitudes to age are very, very good. I was employed into this job at the age of 58 with full benefits, and

I will stay until I retire". A wheelchair user (basic, male), who had just joined the BBC, noted that "they have been phenomenal. The whole site is 'wheelchair user friendly' and they have opened a gym for us on the ground floor with special equipment, etc, and I have meetings with management to see about specific issues to do with my career and any particular problems". These examples serve to illustrate further the general ethos of the BBC. Nonetheless, there were several comments that acknowledged that their racial/ethnicity quotas were lower than they should be. As one senior female manager said: "It is true that we are struggling more on our quotas for ethnic minorities but it is not from lack of trying – but the numbers of applicants from these groups are very low. We have had some bad press on that one and we are really trying to balance it out."

[7] Ten of the 11 female respondents with children, and 8 of the 13 men with children.

[8] Fifteen per cent of engineering undergraduates are female in comparison to 85% male (EOC, 2005).

[9] Hakim goes on to say "This response is consistent with, and supports Goldberg's theory of male dominance. No other theory has been offered which can explain women's rejection of females in authority" (Hakim, 1996, p 119).

[10] Although it should be noted that there are only 4 males within the basic category.

[11] Three females and 2 males from the 'basic' category, and 2 females and 3 males from the 'middle' category. Six of the respondents held first degrees (4 males and 2 females).

[12] Four respondents (2 females and 2 males) replied 'don't know'.

[13] Three respondents said that they 'didn't know' (1 female and 2 males). Only 6 respondents (4 females and 2 males) thought that there was ultimately no process of real change.

FOUR

The 'herding effect'

At this point, then, we can identify the two 'primary causal factors' of VOSS in the BBC study. The first was demonstrated by revealing pervasive biases against women with children. There was evidence that these negative attitudes were rooted in beliefs that women's roles as child bearer and child rearer were unequivocally disruptive to the workplace – making an assumed correlation between mothers' 'domestic commitment' and significantly lower levels of productivity. The second was the substantial practical setbacks that parents faced when trying to combine their domestic and employment responsibilities. This difficulty manifested itself in two notable ways: the problem of arranging affordable childcare for the duration of full working days, and the particular constraints male parents faced in contributing to the routine care of their children. Overall then, two causal interpretations of VOSS emerge from the qualitative data: (1) *stereotypical assumptions* both about mothers' productive capacity in employment and men's routine parenting ability; (2) *structural constraints*, such as institutional policies and practices that inhibit the combination of employment and childcare.

At the end of this chapter we shall return briefly to the 'would be' policy implications of the causal theories we have examined throughout previous chapters. First, however, in a challenge to the claims of these theories, the major contention put forward here is that the *relationship between stereotypical assumptions and structural constraints* should be the focus of our attention if we are to address questions of sex inequality both comprehensively and effectively.

It is well documented that stereotypical assumptions about men and women inhibit sex equality in the workplace. One only needs to scan the feminist canon to find this claim permeating academic discussion[1]. However, this observation alone does not serve as a sufficient causal interpretation of the status quo. Over the following pages the aim is to develop a more subtle account of how such inhibiting stereotypical assumptions are intricately woven into the fabric of VOSS.

In contrast to the causal explanations explored previously – which assume that contemporary lifestyle choices (as indicated by employment trends and domestic arrangements) necessarily reflect 'characteristics of sex' or the subjugation of one sex by the other, it will be argued that there is in fact a specific 'systemic dissonance' between the actual aspirations of individuals in terms of their lifestyles and the possible practical options from which they choose. In other words, that there is a considerable distortion of 'preference' (whether it be women's or men's) in its translation to 'choice' and consequent outcome. This perspective will be explained here, with particular reference to sex equality, using what will be called the 'herding effect of policy'. This concept describes how people are *herded* into particular lifestyle choice-making by virtue of the nature and objectives of current equality laws and policies that directly frame the options from which they are permitted to choose. It is in this sense that much of existing legislation and policy acts, ironically, as a 'structural constraint' to sex equality. The objective over the course of this chapter is to exemplify how current equality principles, laws and policies are largely tethered to anachronistic understandings of 'gender roles' and consequently lag woefully behind the wants and needs of a 21st-century workforce. Central to this perspective is the idea that a circular relationship exists between stereotypes and structural constraints; each appears to justify and mutually perpetuate the other. Such a 'circular perpetuation' goes on to create and to maintain some colossal barriers to equality between men and women, and this is a condition that leaves little room for the future creation of non-discriminatory norms. On this view, it will be suggested that the legal endorsement and subsequent 'exposure' to new and particular egalitarian social arrangements is the fundamental precursor to a state of genuine equality between the sexes, one linked more closely to preferences than to outcomes, and that the promotion of this project therefore should be the normative and practical objective of law makers and policy devisers.

Status quo

Common stereotypical assumptions, which permeate our everyday understandings of how women and men function (and should function) in society, are formidable obstacles to sex equality. As we saw in the context of the BBC, widespread discrimination against female employees by 'managers'[2] derived from the common view that women are more likely to be detrimental to overall workplace productivity, due to their childbearing and childrearing responsibilities. Consequently, many believed that women's lower aggregate position on the 'vertical scale' genuinely reflects lower human capital investment and depressed productivity levels, as argued by proponents of human capital-based theories. This perspective not only offers itself as an explanation for pay and status inequity between the sexes, but more crucially, appears to represent a justification for that inequity.

However, the investigation of this causal interpretation revealed that the BBC respondents' actual lifestyle *choices* clearly did not depend on any difference in the underlying *preferences* of men and women in the workplace. Rather, the respondents themselves directed attention to a series of *structural* factors – factors that shaped the particular work–life choices that they made. Most importantly, the respondents pointed to the overwhelmingly gendered nature of childcare opportunities, especially in the very early stages of childhood. It was not that women as a whole *wanted* to be provided with greater opportunities to opt out of the workforce than men; as was clear from the interviews, the various desires to spend time with children were spread *heterogeneously across both sexes*. Yet the structural opportunities were available *only* to women. There was, that is, a 'systemic dissonance' between the actual aspirations/preferences of female and male workers, and the structured environment in which their work–life balance choices had to be made. Next, we turn to Britain's equality legislation, with special reference to its function as a 'herding agency'.

Equal Treatment Principle

Closely refereed by the EU, the evolution of sex equality legislation in Britain has long been a tumultuous process (see, for example, Meehan, 1985; Fredman, 1997; Deakin and Morris, 1998; and on development of European Law, Hepple, 1995 and 2002). Nevertheless, we have now enjoyed over 30 years of laws specifically designed to equalise the conditions and pay of men and women. As British law currently stands, the primary approach to combating inequality in employment is determined by the Equal Treatment Principle (ETP), as defined by the EU's Equal Treatment Directive (ETD) 2002/73/EC[3].

The ETD's (Article 2) definition of the ETP is "that there shall be no discrimination whatsoever on the grounds of sex either directly or indirectly by reference in particular to marital or family status". Thus, under the directive, discrimination is divided into two concepts: *direct discrimination*, "where one person is treated less favourably on grounds of sex than another is, has been or would be treated in a comparable situation"; and *indirect discrimination*, "where an apparently neutral provision, criterion or practice would put persons of one sex at a particular disadvantage compared with persons of the other sex, unless that provision, criterion or practice is objectively justified by a legitimate aim, and the means of achieving that aim are appropriate and necessary".

The original intent of this approach was to enforce 'blindness' to certain basic characteristics such as 'race' or sex, so that one could not be discriminated against merely on these grounds. For example, since the 1990 *Dekker* case (*Elisabeth Johanna Pacifica Dekker v Stichting Vormingscentrum voor Jong Volwassenen (VJV-Centrum) Plus) Case C-177/88*), an employer is deemed to be in direct contravention of the ETP "if he refuses access to employment, vocational training, promotion, or working conditions [or] refuses to enter into a contract with a female candidate whom he considers to be suitable for the job where such refusal is based on the possible adverse consequences for him of employing a pregnant woman". The ETP, as defined by the ETD, underpins the two primary pieces of anti-sex discrimination law in Britain: the Equal Pay Act and the Sex Discrimination Act.

1970 Equal Pay Act[4]

To contextualise the function of this particular Act it is useful to note that the pay gap between men and women in Britain has stood at approximately 18% for full-time workers for over 20 years and a staggering 40% for part-time workers[5] (EOC, 2005, p 1).

The Equal Pay Act (EqPA) was designed to eradicate unequal rates of pay and contractual conditions between individual men and women in comparable employment. Any person bringing forward a complaint (the complainant) of unequal pay under the Act is required to find an *actual* comparator of the opposite sex in the same employing institution. When the Act was introduced in 1970[6], it required "equal treatment" for men and women only in two distinct situations: either when employed in "like work", which is defined as "the same" or "broadly similar", or when employed in work that had been rated as equivalent by a job evaluation conducted by the employer (EqPA 1970, section 1(2)(a)). However, employers were not obligated to undertake such evaluations. With little incentive to monitor the inequities between men and women's pay, comparisons of individuals' terms of employment were less than reliable (Hepple, 1984). In response to a ruling by the EU, the UK enacted the Equal Value Amendment (EVA) in 1983 so that, since then, the Act applies to a situation where there is work of 'equal value', thereby widening the interpretive scope of comparability.

However, despite the 1983 amendment, the problem of how to motivate less than willing employers to investigate pay differentials remained unsolved. Indicative of this difficulty are the unsavoury results revealed by extensive research by the Equal Opportunities Commission (EOC), which investigated the usage of internal pay audits within British organisations (Neathey et al, 2003). While the majority of employers (54% of large and 67% of medium-sized employers) maintained they had comprehensive measures in place to ensure that women and men received equal pay, they had no plans to conduct pay audits (one can only wonder what were considered 'comprehensive measures'). Only 18% of large employers and 10% of medium-sized employers have actually carried out any sort of pay review and, where pay gaps were found, they were often considerable, in some cases as much as 40%. Even armed with the relevant information, a complainant can only hope to establish 'work rated equivalence' under the EqPA if both her job and the job of her comparator were rated as equivalent under the *same* employer review (see IRS Employment Review, 2004a).

Perhaps the most objectionable finding, however, was that a fifth of all employers (22%) explicitly prohibited employees from sharing with each other any information relating to the details of their earnings. This means that not only is it extremely difficult to ascertain whether one is being paid a lower rate than the 'going market rate', but it also precludes the possibility of formally identifying a comparator, even if relevant information has been shared 'illicitly'[8]. It seems a little ironic, then, that even Patricia Hewitt (Secretary of State for Trade and Industry and Minister for Women from 1999 to 2005) said of this particular EOC report, "this research reveals a depressing snapshot that shows too many workplaces are still stacked against women fulfilling their true earning potential" (EOC, 2003). It would seem, therefore, that the EqPA is far less effective than we first might hope. But the EqPA's limitations do not end with failing to secure that investigative internal pay audits are carried out. Further procedural shortcomings of the EqPA, which diminish its impact on inequality, include the following:

1 The Act only establishes the right to contractual and pay equality with a specific comparator. Each case brought forward to tribunal is treated individually, and, if successful, does not technically apply to colleagues in the same position as the complainant[9]. Trade unions and the EOC are not able to take group or representative action on behalf of similarly affected individuals. Therefore, it can take years to achieve equal pay, and the wider impact of ensuring sex equality in this way may be seriously limited.

2 In cases where the tribunal has commissioned an investigation into a complainant's claims[10], the independent panel appointed by the

Advisory, Conciliation and Arbitration Service (ACAS) consists of only 12 part-time assessors. Thus it is not surprising that the assessment process is extremely lengthy and can take up to two years to complete despite the fact that the European Court of Human Rights has made it clear that undue delay is a contravention of the right to a fair hearing under Article 6 (Rubenstein, 2004, p 23). This onerous procedure undoubtedly represents a significant disincentive for many potential complainants, particularly for those who are in low-paid, low-status positions and who also may feel insecure in their jobs.

3   The EOC supports about 5% of sex discrimination cases each year and trades unions have supported some major, high-profile cases. But, there is no legal aid available to the majority of individual complainants who, even if successful in their claim, have to bear their own legal costs. Again, this will deter many individuals from bringing forward justified grievances, and this is an ironic characteristic of a justice system purportedly orientated toward those in lower paid jobs.

4   The notion of 'proportional equality' is not currently recognised under the EqPA. To illustrate, while a complainant might be able to show that they were paid only 60% of the comparator's wages, the tribunal could deem the complainant's job to be 'worth' 95% of the comparator's job. Under the EqPA there would no grounds for awarding proportional compensation or for setting future proportional remuneration levels. The definition of equality under the EqPA must be *absolute*, irrespective of the degree to which someone is justifiably aggrieved. This form of injustice is a substantial contributor to the pay gap (VOSS). Since the amendments to the ETD (2002/73), there has been some speculation as to whether the new wording might require that proportional equality be upheld in the future[11]. However, when translating the revised directive into UK law, the Department of Trade and Industry (DTI) has ignored this possibility.

5   A defence mechanism available to the employer is that of 'material factors'. These factors may be legally accepted as 'justifiable', non-discriminatory causes of pay disparity between men and women. There are three types: 'labour market factors'; 'organisational factors'; and 'personal factors'. 'Labour market factors' may be invoked in the case of labour shortages, where higher wages may be offered and paid to employees in 'hard to fill' posts. An 'organisational factor' is "a difference which is connected with economic factors affecting the efficient carrying on of the employer's business" (Judgment

held by the House of Lords in *Rainey v Glasgow Health Board*, 1987, cited in Deakin and Morris, 1998, p 645). For example, it may be within an employer's rights to restrict higher paid shift work to full-time employees (the majority of whom might be male) as opposed to (predominantly female) part-time employees. Finally, 'personal factors' can be used to justify differential pay between the complainant and the comparator, based on the comparator's seniority, superior qualifications, or greater productivity. In some cases, of course, these may well be useful ways of classifying acceptable exceptions to the rule. However, as several commentators have pointed out, 'material factors' (including 'personal factors') are open to wide and often dubious interpretations, which can become a fundamental stumbling block to many legitimate claims of injustice (see, for example, Hepple, 1984; Rubenstein, 1984; Fredman, 1997; Deakin and Morris, 1998). In a recent case[12], the Employment Appeal Tribunal held that the employer was not required to produce specific justification for using 'length of service' as a criterion for paying a woman less than her longer-serving male comparators doing equivalent work. Jarman's (1992) research, echoed by the EOC (2005), suggests that female complainants who have taken maternity leave face being ascribed lower 'merit of service', a factor invoked by the employer as a reason to pay women less than men.

6   There are problems of intelligibility. As Lord Denning pointed out, "ordinary individuals who are affected by equal pay for work of equal value ought to be able to read and understand the Regulations. Not one of them would be able to do so. No ordinary lawyer would be able to understand them. The industrial tribunals would have the greatest difficulty and the Court of Appeal would probably be divided in opinion"[13]. Needless to say, it is inexcusable that an Act designed to protect the disadvantaged is unintelligible even to the advisors of those who need to rely on it. Almost 20 years later, the EOC is still campaigning for the government to implement changes to legislation making it more accessible.

7   The EqPA is retrospective rather than pre-emptive in its impact. Even where a complainant's case is successful, there is no legal mechanism in place to ensure that the employer ceases to engage in discriminatory practices. As we have seen, the motivation for employers to act pre-emptively is weak in the context of non-mandatory internal audits, and given the very small number of cases actually won by complainants and the low level of compensation that employers are forced to pay successful complainants. In 2003 the EqPA was amended, granting back pay

of up to six years and, in that year, the median award for sex discrimination was £5,677. While this is an improvement, it hardly serves as a stern warning to employers who contravene the law.

At first sight, then, the EqPA's intention and remit might *seem* logical and straightforward, and it may appear to represent an invaluable aid to those who experience the injustice of labour market exploitation. Yet, on closer inspection, it is quite clearly infused with crude and unwarranted interpretations of 'equal treatment', and considerable disincentives to bring forward claims that render the Act's breadth of impact far from impressive. One need only refer to the pitiful success rate of complainants under the EqPA to bring home this point: between 1976 and 2000 a total of 12,934 complainant applications were made, only 2,540 managed to gain a hearing, and just 641 of these were successful. What is more, it is interesting to note that 25% of tribunal claims end in complete victory for the employer (see IRS Employment Review, 2004b).

1975 Sex Discrimination Act[14]

Unlike the remit of the EqPA (which only allows for claims of unequal pay and contractual terms), the Sex Discrimination Act (SDA) provides for a much more extensive assortment of claims against discrimination, including, for example, the areas of labour market recruitment, promotion and training and termination of employment. Broadly speaking, the purpose of the SDA is to prohibit discrimination on the grounds of sex in employment as well as in areas of education and the provisions of goods (facilities, services and premises to members of the public, and so forth). The Act is not all-embracing; for example, it does not cover those situations where it is considered essential that an employee should be of a particular sex in order to conserve decency or privacy in the workplace, or where one sex is eligible for a specific employment protective right, such as the right for female employees to claim maternity leave when pregnant.

Another problem is that of the burden of proof. Despite the EC Burden of Proof Directive (97/80), which shifts the burden of proof from the complainant to the employer when the complainant has, prima facie, a legitimate claim of unlawful discrimination, there is little evidence that it has become easier for complainants to win their cases of direct discrimination. In cases of direct discrimination, unreasonable behaviour by the employer (related to sex difference) should lead to a straightforward reversal of the burden of proof to the employer. However, proving indirect discrimination can still be very difficult, particularly since workplace statistics are held by the employer[15].

In the end, therefore, the SDA contains many similar practical drawbacks to the EqPA, such as the lengthy assessment procedures and the lack of legal aid for complainants (see for example, EOC Annual Report, 2003). Additionally, it is worth considering one further criticism of the SDA. Although complainants under the SDA, unlike the EqPA, are only required to provide a hypothetical comparator(s), the focus remains on individual disadvantage rather than group disadvantage. It does not automatically follow that a successful case secures the equal treatment of peers under the SDA.

It is evident, overall, that the effectiveness of the EqPA and the SDA as a means with which to combat inequality is highly questionable. Furthermore, the sceptic might argue that their inept design appears to serve an altogether different purpose. It is plausible to claim that legislation equipped with more intrusive and coercive powers would prove intolerable to employers, who insist that such intervention unduly stifles the creative dynamics of the free market, which in turn is claimed to depress the national economy. Accordingly, the very best that can be expected from current arrangements is that the employer is called to award recompense, for it is rare that further punishment will be administered irrespective of the fact that such activities are unlawful. Accordingly there is little (if any) incentive to sustain 'good behaviour'. For example, the EOC's research on employer flexibility for parents indicated that over half the requests for changes to working arrangements were rejected and that around 30,000 working women who were refused alternative working arrangements were either dismissed, made redundant, or forced to resign (EOC, 2005). (It is reported that only 2% of employees who turned to their company's grievance procedures succeeded in getting their proposed working arrangements accepted.) In 2003, the government introduced the right to *request* flexible working arrangements for parents of children under the age of six (or 18 if the child had a disability). There is no *automatic* right to flexible working arrangements under the new provision, however, but it does serve as a reference point for those seeking to facilitate a work–life balance by changing their working arrangements. Whether or not this initiative provides sufficient incentive for employers to overcome their resistance to granting requests remains to be seen.

Specific rights

Moving beyond the two primary British anti-sex discrimination Acts, we find more problems embedded within the interpretation of the ETP in relation to specific employment protection rights for parents ('specific rights'). Unlike either of the anti-sex discrimination Acts, specific rights differ depending on the sex of the employee. Predominantly based on assumptions relating to 'gender roles', it is considered reasonable by the relevant adjudicating bodies to distinguish between men and women in terms of their apparent differing economic needs, as will be illustrated later. This logic, it is argued here, is obstructive, rather than a facilitation of relevant and justified sex equality.

The current array of 'specific rights' available in Britain relate to antenatal care[16] and to maternity leave, paternity leave and parental leave, accompanied with the right to return to one's original place of employment under protection against discrimination.

- *Maternity leave:* since 2003, state-provided standard (or 'ordinary') maternity leave in Britain stands at 26 weeks (including two weeks compulsory protective leave)[17]. This provision stipulates that mothers are entitled to 90% of their usual employment earnings for the first six weeks, followed by 20 weeks at £106 (set in 2005), and a further 26 weeks of unpaid leave, eligibility pending[18].
- *Paternity leave:* finally introduced in Britain in 2003 under EU pressure, this benefit provides two consecutive weeks of paid leave within 56 days of the birth of the child. The rate of statutory pay is akin to maternity leave *after* the first six weeks, £106 per week[19].
- *Parental leave:* in 1999, the EU Parental Leave Directive was implemented in Britain[20]. It offers parents of either sex 13 weeks' leave for each child born after 15 December 1999, available until the child reaches the age of five[21]. As with maternity and paternity leave, the right to return to work after parental leave is guaranteed by law. However, Britain's adoption and interpretation of this directive excluded the statutory provision of *paid* leave and bestowed employers with the power to decide exactly when leave should be taken.

The undoubted improvements introduced by the Labour government notwithstanding, Britain still offers some of the lowest specific parenting benefits in Europe. In terms of maternity leave, for example, pregnant women in Luxembourg are entitled to 16 weeks maternity leave at full pay; in Denmark, 28 weeks at 90% of pay; in Italy 28 weeks at

80% of pay with an optional six months during the child's first year at 30% of pay; in Germany, 15 weeks at full pay; in France, 16 weeks at 84% of earnings; in Belgium, 30 days at 82% and then 75% for a further 15 weeks. The assumption underlying the meagre British provision of six weeks at 90% of average earnings is that women are able to depend on a second wage during the remaining 20 weeks leave (paid at only £106)[22]. It is worth mentioning here the European Court of Justice (ECJ) ruling in the 1996 *Gillespie* case, which stipulated that maternity pay must not be "set so low as to jeopardize the purpose of maternity leave" (*Joan Gillespie and others v Northern Health and Social Services Boards, Department of Health and Social Services Board,* [1996] ECR, p I-00475, para 25). The ruling in this case did make it clear that women on maternity leave were not entitled to full pay, but after the first six weeks of leave each mother is granted only £160 per week in Britain, which if we calculate according to the average full-time worker's 35-hour week, amounts to just £3.03 per hour, thus falling far short of the national minimum wage set at £5.05 per hour, as of October 2005. This means that the average worker, earning £430.93 per week, would lose a hefty £270 of their weekly earnings while on maternity leave. The problem also occurs with paternity leave, which is paid at the same rate but for only two weeks, amounting to a mere 25% of the average paid holiday leave.

These provisions, therefore, are not satisfactory, catering neither for low-income families in particular nor for the demands of modern family life in general. Now that dual-earner and single-parent-headed families are more prevalent than the traditional 'male-breadwinner' model[23], many contemporary families are simply unable to subsist on the meagre benefits available in Britain. Moreover, these inadequate provisions serve to lessen the impact of attitudinal shifts towards more routine fathering (whether economically or psycho-socially motivated). As the qualitative research of BBC workers shows in the previous chapter, the entitlement to unpaid parental leave is no more than a dead letter and, as it currently stands, statutorily provided paid leave relating to childbirth and subsequent care is primarily linked to an employee's physical and social function as 'mother'.

Under the particular interpretation of the ETP as depicted by the ETD, special treatment in favour of pregnant workers is permitted on the view that such special treatment serves to protect them during a vulnerable time. This special treatment clause within the ETP is based on the idea that individuals should only be treated equally in terms of specified relevant respects. The question is, of course, which respects are relevant? Bearing this question in mind, the ETP is particularly awkward in the context of pregnancy where there is no male comparator, and in the context of primary childcare activities where it is *assumed* that there is no male comparator, that is, primary childcare is not considered to be a relevant respect in which men and women should be treated equally in terms of financial provision. The 1984 landmark EJC ruling in the case of *Ulrich Hofmann v Barmer Ersatzkasse*, yet to be superseded, embodies this dilemma. Herr Hofmann (residing in Hamburg, Germany), the father of a newly born baby, claimed that he was being discriminated against on the grounds of sex, because he was denied access to paid benefits, only available to the mother, despite being his child's primary carer. Hofmann's circumstances were such that he had been granted unpaid leave by his employer after the compulsory maternity leave period of eight weeks ended, until the child reached six months of age. During this period, Herr Hofmann was the primary carer of his child as the mother had returned to work. Had the mother availed herself of further statutory maternity leave until the child was six months, she would have been able to claim state-paid benefits of up to DM25 per day. As this was available only to mothers, Hofmann was unable to claim such benefits (*Hofmann case 184/83* [1984] ECR 3047). He argued, therefore, that the German maternity leave provision (*Mutterschutzgesetz*) was in breach of the ETP as defined by the ETD (26/207) and thus also of European Community Law as regards access to employment, vocation training and promotion and working conditions.

In response, however, the EJC ruled that the "Directive 26/207 is not designed to settle questions concerning the organization of the family, or to alter the division of responsibility between parents" (*Hofmann case 184/83* [1984] ECR 3047, summary para 1). This is a stunning statement, since it clearly relies on an a priori notion of what the division of responsibility between parents should be, that is, that only mothers should be primary carers.

Moreover, the ECJ reserved the right of member states to design their own provisions, which are:

> ... intended to protect women in connection with 'pregnancy and maternity'.... Directive 76/207 recognizes the legitimacy, in terms of the principle of equal treatment, of protecting a woman's need in two respects. First, it is legitimate to ensure the protection of a woman's biological condition during pregnancy and thereafter until such time as her physiological and mental functions have returned to normal after childbirth.... Secondly, it is legitimate to

protect the special relationship between a woman and her child over the period which follows pregnancy and childbirth, by preventing that relationship from being disturbed by the multiple burdens which would result from the simultaneous pursuit of employment. (*Hofmann case 184/83* [1984] ECR 3047, summary para 2)

Although the physical trauma of giving birth calls for a compulsory protective period of recovery and recuperation for the mother, it is important to draw attention to the ECJ's comments regarding the return to normal of the mother's "mental functions", and the "special relationship between a women and her child" – these are points to which we shall return in a moment.

The ECJ went on to justify its decision in the following terms;

> ... such leave may legitimately be reserved to the mother to the exclusion of any other person, in view of the fact that it is only the mother who may find herself subject to undesirable pressures to return to work prematurely. (*Hofmann case 184/83* [1984] ECR 3047, summary para 3)

As spelled out here, the ECJ considers that only mothers are "subject to undesirable pressures to return to work" soon after the arrival of a new child. It is then at the discretion of the member states to decide the degree and the nature of protection to be offered to pregnant women or new mothers in order "to offset the disadvantages which women, by comparison with men, suffer with regard to the retention of employment" (*Hofmann case 184/83* [1984] ECR 3047, summary para 4). The fact that fathers may experience the same difficulty in retaining a close bond with the child due to financial and employment obligations during the first few months is simply not considered. Rather, it is stated that "the Directive does not impose on member states a requirement that they shall, as an alternative, allow such leave to be granted to fathers, even where the parents so decide" (*Hofmann case 184/83* [1984] ECR 3047, summary para 5).

The details of Hofmann's complaint are pertinent. He argued, against the interpretation of the ECJ, that the main objective of the leave available to mothers *after* the compulsory maternity leave of eight weeks (two weeks in Britain) until the baby is six months old must be to secure the best interests of the *child* rather than the mother. If indeed this is the case, then there should be grounds on which the father (as well as the mother) may access paid leave provisions, in accordance with the ETP. His claim is based on the following three observations:

- "... the fact that the leave is withdrawn in the event of the child's death ... demonstrates that the leave was created in the interests of the child and not of the mother" (*Hofmann case 184/83* [1984] ECR 3047, objection para 10). This is a particularly relevant point in the context of the ECJ's invocation of "the protection of a woman's biological condition ... until such time as her physiological and mental functions have returned to normal after childbirth". This rationale is used directly as a justification for excluding fathers from access to paid 'maternity' leave beyond the mother's compulsory period of eight weeks in Germany.
- "... the optional nature of the leave [after the compulsory eight weeks] ... means that it cannot be said to have been introduced to meet imperative biological or medical needs" (*Hofmann case 184/83* [1984] ECR 3047, objection para 10). Again, this emphasises the problems of invoking women's physiological and mental condition as a rationale for denying paid leave to fathers post the compulsory period for mothers. Also we might add a criticism here of the ECJ's notion of the "special relationship between a woman and her child". If such a special relationship with the child is only possible with the mother and unquestionably vital to the child's wellbeing, then it does not make sense to make it optional to the mother. Moreover, in the event of the mother opting not to take advantage of this leave, as in the Hoffman case, the ETP would seem to promote the view that *no* parental care is better than paternal care!
- "Lastly, the requirement that the woman should have been employed for a minimum period prior to childbirth; this indicates that it was not considered necessary to grant the leave in the interests of the mother, otherwise it ought to have been extended to all women in employment irrespective of the date on which their employment commenced" (*Hofmann case 184/83* [1984] ECR 3047, objection para 10). Even if, therefore, it cannot be shown that the policy was designed in the best interests of the child, Hofmann's contention is that the policy certainly was not intended to be in the best interests of the mother and again if this is the case the rationale for excluding fathers from paid provision collapses.

According to Hofmann, the protection of the mother against the multiplicity of burdens imposed by motherhood and her employment could be achieved by non-discriminatory measures, such as permitting the father to enjoy the leave with pay thereby creating a period of parental leave after the compulsory maternity leave[24]. That would release the mother from the responsibility of caring for the child, thereby enabling her to resume employment as soon as the compulsory protective maternity leave period had expired. Hofmann also maintained that the available options to parents should be in accordance with the ETP and the choice made in each case be the prerogative of the parents. In this way, moreover, men (as well as women) would be protected from being "subject to undesirable pressures to return to work prematurely".

Hofmann did not win his case in 1984. Yet the logic of his claim still stands up today and it is imperative, I argue here, that we reconsider the dubious reasons for resisting Hofmann's compelling reinterpretation of the ETP. Judging by the comments contained within the European Court reports on Hofmann's case, it seems that the final ruling was an uncomfortable one:

> The Commission draws attention to the fact that, in a number of member states, social legislation is moving towards the grant of 'parental leave' or 'child-care leave' which is to be preferred to leave which is available to the mother alone. It is stated that it was considering whether to bring actions for failure to fulfil a treaty obligation against a number of member states which, in various forms, retained measures which were comparable to the maternity leave provided for by the German legislation. (*Hofmann case 184/ 83* [1984] ECR 3047, grounds para 13)

Certainly, one could argue that political considerations were decisive in this case, for to have fulfilled Hofmann's request would have been tantamount to forcing a member state to radically reconfigure its domestic policy (and if it had, in this case in Germany, it would not have been long before all member states would have had to do the same). This aside, the only other justification for not considering 'paid leave for the purposes of primary childcare' as a relevant respect in which men and women should be treated equally, is one based on stereotypical assumptions about what role men and women should respectively play in the lives of their children. Neither motivation nor justification is warranted. Also, here my previous comments on 'gender' in the Introduction of the book are relevant. In the case of Hofmann, we are concerned with the fact that he should not be discriminated against purely because he is a man; we are not concerned with whether or not he has particular gender characteristics.

Clearly, gestation, parturition and breast-feeding are unique to women (and therefore rightfully protected by compulsory maternity leave) but the exclusive nature of these functions does not extend to 'parenting', which might more usefully be recognised as a shared responsibility of mothers and fathers. This view is echoed in a vast number of case studies. For instance, Burgess (Burgess and Ruxton, 1996; Burgess, 1997), drawing on extensive empirical research in conjunction with a wide-ranging review of numerous similar studies (such as those of Bell, 1983; Colman and Colman, 1988; and Pittmann, 1993), asserts that "what has been shown – and shown over and over again with almost painful ease – is how sex role *conditioning* drives a wedge between men and their parenting instincts" (Burgess, 1997, p 98; emphasis in the original. See also Gregg and Washbrook, 2003)[25].

The biological function to procreate and breast-feed does not secure innately superior parenting skills. Parenting demands a whole of range of abilities (such as the ability to construct imaginative ways of playing, to communicate, to teach, to tend to sickness, to supervise, to dress, to bathe, to put to bed and simply to spend creative time with children), characteristics that, by any account, are not the sole preserve of one particular sex. This point is stressed by Burgess, who contends that parenting styles are determined by situation and not by sex. According to her, when fathers are exposed to the experience of being routine carer, their capacity for tending to children in different contexts is as varied as that of women, ranging from the model parent at one end of the spectrum to the hopelessly inept at the other. Moreover, there is mounting evidence that, given the opportunity, many fathers are in fact demanding to spend more time than ever with their children. This is undoubtedly the result of huge shifts in social attitudes of the new parenting generation and associated changing social norms (see Hatter et al, 2002; O'Brien and Shemilt, 2003; Gregg and Washbrook, 2003).

The likelihood of creating an environment in which parents are able to enact their duties or their express wishes, irrespective of their sex, is largely dependent on the dictates of societal ideals, organisation and legal underpinnings. Unfortunately then, contemporary interpretations of the principle of equal treatment (particularly the way in which the ETD has prescribed the ETP) has shown itself to be limited in this respect by permitting the neglect of the 'male as parent' and in so doing directly perpetuating the stereotypes of 'gender' – a condition Fredman refers to as "rigid role demarcation" (Fredman, 1997, p 206).

There has of course been a recent revolutionary moment in British social policy first referred to in the 2005 *Labour Party Manifesto* (*LPM*), where Blair's government set forth proposals (which one would have to consider radical in the British context) to alter maternity leave provisions in order "to give fathers more opportunities to spend time with their children ... including the option of sharing paid leave" (Labour Party, 2005, ch 6). New policy proposals include the extension of statutory maternity pay to nine months[26] and the right for women to transfer up to six months of their paid maternity leave to fathers during the first year of the child's life from April 2007. These are extremely welcome developments in social policy terms, but once again they contain some serious limitations with unfortunate ramifications and are not in conformity with the principle of equal treatment argued for by Hofmann and advocated here.

Firstly, even with the extension of leave for women, the low statutory pay is a deterrent to most dual-income families. While all the details of this scheme are yet to be fleshed out it looks likely that the new transferable leave will be available to the father *only* after three months of the mother's maternity leave. One feature that is certain, however, is that fathers will only be entitled to the statutory flat rate maternity pay (currently set at £106 per week), on which it is extremely difficult for families to rely for any sustained period even as an income secondary to the average wage.

Secondly, the parents of a child are not allowed to take their leave simultaneously. The idea is that only when the mother returns to work will the father be able to begin his period of transferred leave (having exhausted his statutory paternity leave of two weeks), so that the total period of leave taken is continuous. For many parents, alternative arrangements might better suit their needs; for example, both might wish to take part-time leave simultaneously. This might be a much more reasonable financial arrangement for many families, where a pro-rata part-time wage in addition to half the statutory maternity pay would enable (and encourage) families to take the leave available to them without seriously jeopardising their economic stability[27]. Furthermore, this arrangement would be more in line with an interpretation of the Equal Treatment Principle that would not be based on gender role stereotypes.

In addition, demographic changes and the ever-growing concern that the next generation will not be financially self-sufficient in old age, should be an economic motivator for politicians to promote the extension of paid parental/maternity leave to both parents (excluding the compulsory period only). Such provisions would invariably enable more women to remain in the labour market full time and vitally, to prepare for their old age with occupational pensions. This is a long-term and very important concern for both individuals and the state when we consider that people aged 85 and over are the fastest growing age group in the British population. There are now 18 times as many 'over-85s' – referred to by the Office for National Statistics (ONS) as the 'oldest old' – as there were in 1901 (1,104,000 compared with 61,000), and this figure is expected to more than double to 2,479,000 by 2031. What is more, for every man there are currently 257 women in this age group (ONS, 2005a). In terms of the wider group of 11 million pensioners (those aged over 65), 63% (6.93 million) are women. The average income of women in retirement is just 57% that of retired men. Only 13% (1.43 million) of women pensioners receive a full basic state pension based on their own national insurance contribution[28].

Only 56% of working women are employed full time, earning, as mentioned earlier, an average of 18% less than men (and 40% less for the 43% who work part time). Of these, only 38% of working women are members of an occupational pension scheme. Consequently, according to the National Pensioners' Convention, one in four older women live below the poverty line and two out of every three of the pensioners who claim means-tested support are women. These alarming trends coincide with the fact that the first few years of the 21st century saw the lowest ever birth rate in the history of Britain (ONS, 2005b). Currently, the average income for a pension household is £12,400, which is less than half the national average wage, with 2.2 million pensioners living below the official poverty line (Brewer et al, 2005).

Indicative of the growing concern among European governments regarding top heavy demographic trends, the French Prime Minister (2005-), Dominique de Villepin, has recently vouched to pay mothers £507 per month, for up to a year, for every *third* child born in order to provide an incentive for French parents to have more children – despite France already having the second highest birth rate in Europe. Similarly, demographic concerns provided the rationale behind Sweden's policy to encourage higher birth rates. Generally regarded as one of the most advanced, family-friendly schemes in the world, Sweden pioneered paid maternity leave in 1955, which it later converted into paid parental leave in 1974. Given the extensions to the paid parental scheme over the past two decades (currently paid at a high rate of income replacement by the state of 80% of earnings and accompanied by the right to return to employment with protection against discrimination)[29], it is no surprise that Sweden has the highest female economic activity rates (82.6%), the third highest fertility rate in Europe after Ireland[30] and France, and enjoys the highest male take-up rates (77%) for parental leave in Europe (see O'Brien and Shemilt, 2003; Haas and Hwang, 2005).

The gender stereotypes on which British policy provision judgements are currently made not only deny men the plausible opportunity of becoming active routine parents (with regard to the issue of pay) but also consequently designate the role of primary carer to women, regardless of the psycho-social preferences or economic needs of the individuals in question. Such judgements and the resulting character of state provision have had enormous impact on the general structure of society and the interrelated lifestyle choices that people have no option but to make vis-a-vis their employment trajectories and domestic arrangements. The particular interpretation of the principle of equal treatment discussed in this chapter has instigated misshapen policies that act to 'herd' individuals into self-fulfilling and self-perpetuating stereotypical roles. Although of course some people's choices may indeed coincide with expressed preferences that pertain to 'gender', the 'herding effect' nevertheless sustains the robust nature of the status quo in contemporary society, replete with unnecessary demarcations along the lines of sex.

Wider policies

"The strength of one's *rights* should not be over-estimated....
They rely almost entirely on the individual's enforcement
in a judicial system which is ridden with deterrents."
(Fredman, 1997, p 415)

Many have illustrated that although the law as it stands has improved women's involvement in the labour market, it has done so "without significantly altering the domestic division of labour" (Charles, 1993, p 250; see also Crompton, forthcoming: 2007). Granting the majority of (limited) rights to mothers, rather than to both mothers *and* fathers, only serves to perpetuate stereotypical gender dynamics. And, as the interviews with BBC staff clearly revealed, it is these kinds of assumptions that sustain negative and biased attitudes towards women in the workplace, while also hindering men's attempts to become more active in the routine parenting of their children.

Childcare provision

The BBC staff interviews further illustrated not only that the provisions under specific rights are limited in their scope, but also that the serious lack of affordable childcare facilities represents yet another obstacle to combining work with parenting. In Britain, only 5% of employers provide any sort of childcare services or contributions to childcare costs outside of the workplace (Daycare Trust, 2001). Moreover, although the BBC is certainly more generous than most employers with respect to its childcare provisions, its staff suggested that employers are not the best providers of such services, as they are unable to cater to more than a fraction of those who are really in need of it.

As British law currently stands, there is no provision of comprehensive state childcare. The National Childcare Strategy was introduced by New Labour in 1998, with the intention of encouraging the growth of local, affordable childcare provision for children up to the age of 14 within every community, focusing in particular on the 250 most deprived areas in the UK. Under the auspices of this policy programme, the 'Sure Start for Every Child' campaign was introduced to encourage the growth of childminding businesses and crèches across Britain (particularly in the most deprived areas). This campaign, with an initial budget of £450 million per annum, offers the chance for individuals, community collectives, social entrepreneurs and so forth to bid for start-up grants and, if successful, they are granted registered professional status. While this does constitute an important improvement, with 524 Sure Start Local Programmes resulting in an increase of 525,000 childcare places since 1998 (DTI, 2005), there is still only one childcare place for every four children under the age of eight in the UK as a whole according to the Daycare Trust (2005b). Furthermore, despite Sure Start initiatives, such as some free part-time childcare for children between the ages of three and five[31], British parents still face the highest childcare costs in Europe. For example, the average cost of such services is £141 a week in England, amounting to £7,300 a year. Due to the severe shortage of places, the price of provision is continuing to rise sharply; since 2003, the average cost has increased by 5.2%, which is three-and-a-quarter times the rate of inflation[32]. In some places, most notably London, the costs are considerably higher and typically range from between £197 to £350 per week, amounting to a staggering £10,000 to £18,000 a year[33].

The high cost of childcare in Britain might explain why only 13% of parents with dependent children use formal childcare services all the time. The lack of high quality, easily accessible childcare is obviously a major obstacle to those who attempt to combine having children with jobs and is likely to be the main reason why Britain has one of the lowest economic activity rates for mothers of young children in Europe, particularly for single mothers (Daycare Trust, 2005c).

Tax credits

Under the 'welfare policy approach' (a motif of the Blair administration), there have been some attempts to counteract the problem of expensive childcare for low-income parents in the form of tax credit systems. This type of indirect benefit, favoured over the direct provision of financial aid and state-provided services, is generally aimed at encouraging people into paid employment. In 2003, the old Working Family Tax Credit was substituted with two new systems, the Child Tax Credit and the Working Tax Credit[34].

Child Tax Credit: this is designed for couples whose combined income is less than £58,000 per annum, irrespective of employment status[35] and it is paid directly to the primary carer. A 'family element' of £545 is paid per annum and is doubled to £1,090 in the financial year of a child's birth for one year. All families with incomes of less than £50,000 are guaranteed at least £545 from this element. Should the couple's combined income be less than £13,320 per annum then they will receive an additional 'child element' of £1,625 per annum for each child (and this benefit is offered at different rates according to level of income).

Working Tax Credit: this is not aimed only at parents, but it does include a 'childcare element' for those families in which a lone parent or both partners work a minimum of 16 hours per week. Up to 70% of childcare costs[36] to a maximum of £200 a week can be obtained by parents of two children, and a maximum £135 is available for parents of one child.

Again, there is little doubt that these tax credit systems do represent an improvement on previous provisions. Nonetheless, they do not go far enough to tackle the problems of working parents. Indeed, many commentators have expressed disappointment at the Blair administration's approach to these issues. Among others, the EOC, the Daycare Trust, the National Council for One Parent Families, and the Chartered Institute of Personnel and Development (CIPD) have pointed to the extremely low take-up rates of the childcare element of the Working Tax Credit system (only around 2.3% of parents with dependent children). Moreover, despite the plan to encourage people into paid work by integrating benefits into the tax system instead of providing direct 'hand-outs', 22% of parents with an annual income below £20,000 have given up paid employment due to the difficulties of paying for childcare. Indeed, despite New Labour's claims to have created a 'New Deal for Lone Parents'[37], 44% of lone-parent families are currently out of work (ONS, 2005b).

Given that a maximum of 70% of childcare costs are available to claimants, it is arguably unreasonable to expect all lone parents to fund 30% of their childcare costs, given that the majority are among the lowest national earners. Another more general problem is that the childcare element can only be claimed for the use of registered childcare. Many single-parent families make use of informal, unregistered care and are therefore not entitled to receive the tax credit. All in all, the current average award through the childcare element of the Working Tax Credit is £49.83 per week. Those with more than two children are still only entitled to a maximum of £200 per week (and only if the combined salary is under £13,910 per annum). These are low figures, considering the average costs of childcare. Even the average worker, earning £430.93 per week (£22,411 per annum) would struggle to pay for standard childcare, which certainly does not bode well for low-income families.

Soft law: an emerging approach

Over the past decade there has been a proliferation of best practice codes and expanded models of corporate governance. Labelled 'soft law', these guides for voluntary action are increasingly offered as substitutes for conventional, state-centred, 'hard' social policy, with the intention of remedying such social ills as the pay gap between men and women (see Bartlett et al, 1998; White, 2001; Hepple, 2002; Jenkins et al, 2002). A recent example is the Kingsmill Review (2001), the latest Cabinet Office review on women's employment and pay, widely regarded as marking a significant moment in the development of New Labour's approach to 'gender inequality'.

The Kingsmill Review was modelled on a series of high-profile corporate governance reports, such as the Cadbury Report (1992)[38], the Turnbull Report (1999)[39], and the Company Law Review (2001)[40], all of which were designed to promote a distinctive agenda of 'corporate social responsibility' by means of various internal accountability and disclosure mechanisms (Browne et al, 2005, see also Browne, 2004).

But Kingsmill differed from these previous models in one fundamental respect. For, while these earlier reviews had been designed neither to tackle, nor even to focus on, specific socioeconomic problems, the Kingsmill Review attempted to combine the primary corporate objectives of 'minimising risk' and 'enhancing returns', with an inquiry into a specific problem in social policy, that of VOSS. The Cabinet Office specifically requested that the Review team identify "non-legislative and cost-effective" solutions to the pay gap between men and women (Kingsmill, 2001, p 149). As such, the Review explicitly sought, as the Minister for Women, Barbara Roche, put it, to connect a specific "social injustice with an economic rationale to eradicate it" (Treanor, *Guardian*, 2001).

Thus, instead of calling for any additional state-centred programmes of regulation or provision, the Review recommended that employing corporations should be asked to conduct internal pay reviews, with a particular focus on 'gendered employment patterns'. The purpose of these pay reviews was to ensure the emergence of a much needed comparable dataset across employing organisations in the British labour market. This, in turn, was designed to facilitate a clearer indication of how corporations were addressing issues of VOSS and whether they were guilty of mismanagement and under-utilisation of female human capital. It was argued that with such information disclosed, corporations would become aware of their failings and consequently address them (or be pressurised to do so), thereby reducing the pay gap without the need for interventionist legislation or regulation.

In order to investigate the causes of the pay gap (VOSS), the Kingsmill Review interviewed representatives of 50 of the largest corporations based in Britain. Reflecting on the findings of those who had done some investigative work into the sex distribution across occupations, the Review concluded that VOSS was not primarily a result of unlawful wage inequality, but rather – akin to the BBC study – it was a product of "the clustering of women in lower paid and lower status roles within firms" (Kingsmill, 2001, p 53). Using one particular organisation as an indicator of general trends, it was shown that:

> ... a high proportion of women were remaining static within the organization while the men moved through to higher grades. This presented a business problem both because it was felt that many of the women were operating below their potential and thus depriving the company of valuable skills and expertise and that such stasis ... impeded

the promotion opportunities for those below them in the organization. (Kingsmill, 2001, p 52)

Based on such evidence, the Kingsmill Review developed its recommendations for better human resource management, claiming that this was the locus of the problem. The call for greater transparency and disclosure in terms of gendered pay differences within organisations was considered the most important single recommendation, simultaneously being of the greatest value to the business case, and offering the most likely apparent solution to the persistence of VOSS:

> The driver of the virtuous circle in which business incentives prompt a strategy to promote diversity, which in turn deliver greater profits, is *information*. This means information and quantitative data available at the firm level to generate both an understanding of where best practice lies, and a situation in which those firms which are getting their human capital management right are rewarded through higher levels of investor confidence and ultimately high shareholder value. (Kingsmill, 2001, p 51)

The generation of such information would take the form of internal pay reviews with a particular focus on gender differences in employment. The Review's recommendation for internal audits was pitched in terms of the human capital management practices necessary to aid the efficient and well-considered allocation of resources by investors and shareholders. This, in turn, would reduce three major types of *risk* and *costs* to organisations: first, 'reputational damage' (including loss of investor confidence, loss of shareholder confidence and loss of consumer base); second, the potential litigation brought forward by those claiming unequal pay with the opposite sex; and third, the risk and cost of the inability to recruit and maintain high calibre employees on the basis of being an unsavoury working environment. This is an ideology of optimal market competition. While the motivation is still focused on maximising efficiency and profit, Kingsmill argued that there is a need to broaden our understanding of the means necessary for the effective pursuit of those goals. The gathering of better information should enable effective human capital management to 'drive out' sex discrimination in the interests of corporate self-interest (for further discussion, see Sunstein, 1997).

The Review assumed that the government could put pressure on the public sector to conform to its recommendations, and, that there would be a general campaign to encourage private sector firms to conduct similar reviews, in the hope that being publicly 'named and shamed' for failing to do so would act as a sufficient incentive.

As the current situation stands, although 'gender' is technically present in many business annual reports or voluntary reviews, the analysis is invariably of a very poor quality and content is far from consistent across organisations. There is no doubt that the 'Kingsmill audits', if well administered, would provide invaluable information about occupational sex segregation and the impact of equality policy. However, it is unlikely that this approach is actually *sufficient* to tackle the problems of the pay gap between men and women, given the legal and policy shortcomings so far discussed.

Like the empirical study central to this book, the Review identified the BBC as a model employer and one that had already done much to achieve the goals recommended by the Review. In implementing progressive equality policies and human resource management, the BBC was seen to demonstrate an extremely high level of competency. Yet, as illustrated in the previous chapters, although some very encouraging results are apparent in the higher paying occupations (and the business case for reducing VOSS is widely accepted as motivating the corporation's positive attitude to women's employment), there were also some troubling results related to the lower grade female-dominated jobs, and it was clear from the qualitative data that these problems were generated by more substantial issues than a mere lack of reporting. Employers and managers still face the reality of short-term budgetary concerns while operating within a national employment framework that is both ill-conceived and constraining. Moreover, while organisations may well be persuaded to introduce women into the higher levels of employment hierarchies (as in the case of the BBC), the greatest problem lies with the women concentrated in the lower paid jobs, where 'the business case' for developing human capital is likely to be less compelling. Therefore, such a disparity between women's and men's employment prospects (and the consequent trend of VOSS) seems likely to persist unless the factors impeding women's promotion from the lower end of the employment structure are also adequately addressed.

Hence, the soft law option is a welcome addition to the field, but it is no substitute for progressive policy. Despite governmental enthusiasm for this sort of approach, not least marked by a £1.5 million Work–Life Balance Challenge Fund introduced in 2000 to help employers develop work–life balance practices (Millar and Ridge, 2002), the authors of corporate governance are subject only to persuasion and not to enforcement, and neither the state nor the individual has recourse to binding measures (see Hepple, 2002). These limitations notwithstanding, the recommendations of the Kingsmill Review are clearly important. Social policy strategists and academics are in *dire need* of the invaluable informational base that would be generated by the proposed pay audits from all sectors of the labour force. It is disappointing, therefore, as the EOC has pointed out, that over two thirds of UK organisations (68%) had not conducted any sort of equal pay review and did not intend to do so[41]. Indeed, the highly publicised Kingsmill Review itself focused on 50 organisations, only nine of which agreed to undertake the specific internal reviews recommended, despite being under the media spotlight. Ironically, this example of intransigence casts serious doubt on the viability of the so-called 'name and shame' approach, on which the Review's recommendations largely depend. The mere threat of reputational cost, therefore, seems unlikely to secure the intended changes in the immediate future.

Of course Britain is not the only country to face this problem and it is possible to find alternative approaches in other countries. Under the 1991 Equal Opportunities Act (EOA) in Sweden, for example, employers with 10 or more employees must produce an annual strategy report for ensuring sex equality at work. One compulsory feature of the report is a detailed plan of how best to facilitate the combination of employment and parenthood for female and male employees. It must also include an assessment of the current state of affairs and the results of the previous year's plan, as well as specific prescriptions for the following year, which must be focused on quantifiable goals. Moreover, the Swedish equal opportunities ombudsman monitors these strategies and has the authority to introduce investigations into employers' procedures, to establish the degree of non-compliance with the EOA. Clearly, by putting the onus on the employer to comply with such an annual obligation, the capacity to monitor and assess the achievement of policy goals indisputably is improved.

Direction of policy

As Lewis (2002) shows, pre-New Labour policy focused solely on fathers' financial responsibilities to children and consequently effected the reinforcement of traditional gender roles rather than enabling fathers to develop a caring role. Motivated by the highest divorce rate in Europe and one of the fastest growth rates in unmarried motherhood, British policy makers had previously sought to ensure fathers' financial commitment to their families by means of punitive forms of legislation (as aided by the investigative powers of the National Childcare Agency). However, as noted in this chapter, the Labour government has substantially revised social policy regarding parents of both sexes. It is certainly fair to say that this government is uniquely progressive in its attempts to tighten the relationship between the realm of the family and the state, claiming that previous administrations did not tackle these problems for "fear of seeming to 'nanny'" the British population (Labour Party, 2005, ch 6). Now that the Labour Party has secured a third term in office, it is apparent from the 2005 Manifesto that schemes such as tax credits and the National Childcare Strategy remain at the core of government 'family policy' objectives. The current administration is keen to reconfigure its policies as positively 'family-friendly', with a constant focus on enabling parents to seek and remain in employment while juggling childcare responsibilities. The new proposals to transfer some maternity leave to fathers, despite substantial shortcomings, does mark a monumental shift in the institutional perspective on sex equality but still, and in fact vitally, the particular interpretation of what should be the 'relevant respects' in which men and women are to be treated equally, if they so wish, remains far wide of the mark and will invariably scupper the opportunity to further genuine and justified equality. Policies based on an inadequate interpretation of what the sexes are capable of (and consequently of what they are entitled to be treated equally in) only serve to create a cul-de-sac of social norms with little potential for progressive change. We have seen here how various policies herd individuals into stereotypical roles. Until this changes, 'the stereotype' will robustly legitimise inequality.

Policy implications of causal theories of VOSS

In this chapter thus far, we have seen the ways in which the law and policy approaches rely on particular understandings of how men and women operate in and between home life and work. Now we shall return briefly to the claims made by the three explanatory theories of VOSS and survey how various scholars have attempted to explore the legal, policy and institutional ramifications of these theories. The purpose of this exercise is to outline how the shortcomings of these various theoretical approaches set out in Chapter One continue to limit their efficacy as guides to policy.

Binary-based theories

Bartlett (1990), Cahn (1991) and Menkel-Meadow (1987) use Gilligan's (1982/93) ideas that men and women operate according to different moral codes to analyse the mechanisms of law and connected political institutions. They argue that such mechanisms are biased against women in that they are constructed according to the male morality of autonomy, individualism and abstract rights and duties. Consequently, the female morality of caring, intimacy, connection and a focus on relationships is not similarly represented and that this is to the extensive detriment of women. These theorists' views on legal and political reform are that 'female values' should be influential throughout institutional systems. Rather than focusing on the remits and provisions of specific laws and policies, these theorists' main argument is that the 'female voice' should be strengthened in the legal system, thereby increasing the recognition of specific female experiences. For example, Menkel-Meadow (1987) suggests that rather than using the notion of adversarial court procedures and litigation, legal practice should incorporate a notion of mediation – which she sees as a particular female skill. She states:

> The growing strength of women's voice in the legal profession may change the adversarial system into a more co-operative, less war-like system of communication between disputants in which solutions are mutually agreed rather than dictated by an outsider, won by the victor and imposed upon the loser. (Menkel-Meadow, 1987, pp 54-5)

It is not clear from this account, however, whether the use of 'female approaches' to law is deemed suitable only for female disputants. To follow the logic of Menkel-Meadow's argument, 'female values' would be forced on men who are seen to hold distinct 'male values'. This imposition would presumably be unsuitable for cases centred on the objective of sex equality itself.

Psycho-physiological accounts of sex difference do not offer us any constructive way forward in terms of rectifying injustices through law, policy or politics. As was explored in Chapter One, Goldberg's Male Dominance Theory asserts that social inequality between men and women is a reflection of innate differences. Baron-Cohen, meanwhile, very rarely makes any comments on how we should address the social consequences of his findings. It is interesting to note, however, when asked to explore the ramifications of his work by an influential scientific website-based discussion forum, the speculations he offered might well stand as a commentary on the work of Gilligan.

> What would it be like if our political chambers were based on the principles of empathizing?.... Gone would be politicians who are skilled orators but who simply deliver monologues, standing on a platform, pointing forcefully into the air to underline their insistence – even the body language containing an implied threat of poking their listener in the chest or the face – to win over an audience. Gone too would be politicians who are so principled that they are rigid and uncompromising. Instead, we would elect politicians based on different qualities: politicians who are good listeners, who ask questions of others instead of assuming they know the right course of action. We would instead have politicians who respond sensitively to one another ... who can be flexible over where the dialogue might lead. Instead of seeking to control and dominate, our politicians would be seeking to support, enable, and care. (Baron-Cohen, 2006)

Baron-Cohen's playful tone only serves to underline the remoteness of this approach to political representation as a plausible prospect.

Theories of patriarchy

In conjunction with theories of patriarchy, many legal theorists identify the law as: "maintaining male domination" (Polan, 1982, p 294); "a paradigm of maleness" (Rifkin, 1980, p 84); and "a powerful conduit for the reproduction and transmission of the dominant ideology" (Thornton, 1986, p 5). These writers reject perspectives based on Gilligan's dichotomy of gendered morality. They argue that attempts to insert 'different female values' into the law will only serve to reinforce gender binaries that fortify the subordinating powers of patriarchy. As MacKinnon famously argued in a dialogue with Gilligan, a woman cannot speak for herself as man's "foot is on her throat" (see Benhabib, 1994). As with the binary-based theorists, specific laws and policies concerned with sex equality are not the primary focus of the patriarchy theorists. Their central argument is that to accept 'the male' as the invariable benchmark by which equality between the sexes is measured counteracts the very notion of equality. Accordingly, the use of the law as a tool for emancipation only serves to solidify the subjugating social norms (MacKinnon, 1983) and merely reproduces, rather than diminishes, patriarchal power relations (Thornton, 1986).

Certainly, it is reasonable to argue that the constructed 'male norm' is disadvantageous to women. However, as we saw in previous chapters, the patriarchal theorists themselves construct a stereotype of 'the male norm' that is disadvantageous to both women *and men*. Ultimately, they do not differ from the binary-based approaches. While it is the case that such stereotypes are prevalent in legal practice, the patriarchy theorists are ironically themselves guilty of sustaining them. And in assessing these perspectives, it is not clear what a plausible 'way forward' would be in terms of combating sex inequality.

Bryson (forthcoming: 2007) worries that the equal rights discourse, with its focus on the individual, obscures the disadvantage of women as a group. She insists that we must view society as patriarchal in order to see how best to bring about sex equality. However, if we are to move beyond institutional biases we first have to concede our own. The theory of patriarchy is too blunt an instrument with which to address the questions raised by, for example, the Hofmann case elaborated earlier. Indeed the stereotypes of both men and society at the root of Patriarchy Theory risk impeding rather than promoting sex equality.

Human capital-based theories

Human capital-based accounts of sex inequality account for some of the most influential approaches in legal theory and demand a little more attention than the previous two theoretical approaches. Similar to Becker's Rational Choice Theory, Posner's (1992) theory of household production asserts that women and men yield 'gains from specialisation' in that the man maximises the family's income by specialising in the labour market while the woman "maximises the value of her time as an input into the production of the household's output" (Posner, 1992, p 142).

However (like Hakim), he then goes on to concede that such a rigid dichotomy between male and female specialisations is an 'exaggeration' in the contemporary context in which women's share in the labour market has vastly increased over the past three decades. Posner argues, however, that the reason for identifying the traditional nuclear model of the family as a useful starting point is that people continue, by and large, to adhere to sex-role specialisations and expectations within households and the workplace. This, Posner argues, (like Becker) is primarily because of women's unique altruistic relationship to childcare and as a consequence, their lower acquisition of human capital.

Posner claims not to deny the existence of sex discrimination but then goes on to assert that legislating structural measures to aid women's activity in the labour market, is inefficient and a waste of public revenue:

> ... not all discrimination is inefficient ... therefore efforts to prevent it impose a social cost over and above the cost of the efforts themselves. An example of efficient discrimination in the area of sex is the refusal (which is now unlawful) of employers to pay pregnancy disability benefits. From the employer's standpoint, and also from the standpoint of the efficient pricing of labor, to pay a worker who is absent on account of pregnancy makes no more sense than to pay a worker who is absent because he is nursing a hangover. (Posner, 1992, p 337)

Posner also condemns the principle of paying men and women for work of 'comparable worth' (the US equivalent of 'work of equal value' in the 1970 EqPA). He argues that the implementation of the principle of 'comparable worth' is in fact to artificially inflate the wages of women, which can only result in economic inefficiency and moreover provides no incentive for women to make concerted efforts to increase their human capital levels. Most radically perhaps, Posner argues that legal intervention into 'the market' is detrimental to all concerned:

> ... the added costs, both direct and indirect, that anti-discrimination laws impose on employers will be passed on in part to consumers, in the form of higher prices – and female consumers will be hurt along with male. The heterogeneity of women's interests, combined with the financial and altruistic interdependence between men and women, makes it still more uncertain that women will be net beneficiaries of anti-discrimination laws. Take pregnancy disability benefits again. If employers are forced to provide these benefits, their labor costs will be higher, and this will lead them to employ fewer workers, pay lower wages, and charge higher prices. These costs will fall on both men and women ... all consumers will have to pay higher prices if

labor inputs are used less efficiently as a result of the outlawing of efficient discrimination. (Posner, 1992, p 338)

Posner's work provides a clear example of how human capital-based theories support neoliberal approaches to the role of state provision. Although not opposed to anti-sex discrimination legislation, Hakim (1996, 1999, forthcoming: 2007) similarly argues that legislation since the 1970s has been effective in addressing discrimination and that the residual levels of VOSS are set to persist:

Preference theory predicts men will retain their dominance in the labour market, politics and other competitive activities, because only a minority of women are prepared to prioritise their jobs (or other activities in the public sphere) in the same way as men. (Hakim, forthcoming: 2007)

Hakim further criticises the 'comparable worth' principle adopted by US anti-sex discrimination legislation. In assessing the usefulness of 'comparable worth', Hakim (1996, p 196) claims that such policies "were introduced in the USA as a result of faulty social science evidence". She recounts how in the late 1970s, the Equal Employment Opportunity Commission (EEOC) sought to decrease the stark pay disparity between men and women in the US's labour market and consequently requested an official report on the pay gap between men and women (see Treiman and Hartmann, 1981). The report concluded that discriminatory procedures were to blame, and that to pay men and women equally for doing jobs of 'comparable worth' was the solution, a conclusion that resulted in the general adoption of pay systems based on the 'comparable worth' principle (much like the 1982 amendment to the 1970 EqPA, which encompassed the 'equal value' principle). Hakim (1996, p 197) maintains, however, that while women's jobs may have been undervalued, that it was "wrong to conclude that discrimination was a more important explanatory factor than human capital variables". In this account such legislation interference merely distorts the 'real' effects of human capital differences between men and women:

Female heterogeneity can no longer be ignored as it is the source of increasing polarisation within the female workforce, and has social and economic consequences that are not affected by sex discrimination legislation. (Hakim, 1996, p 207)

Nevertheless, the case of the BBC demonstrates that *extended* provision enabling both women *and* men to combine parenthood and employment is highly likely to be a sine qua non for the reduction in the pay gap between the sexes. Moreover, the provision of a wider set of practical options should not be understood merely as meddling with the natural outcomes of predictable preferences (as Hakim and Posner both seem to suggest) but rather, as the Hofmann case exemplifies, the facilitation of genuine lifestyle choices currently restricted by outdated readings of the capabilities and preferences of each sex.

Hakim, adamant that sex differences in work orientations and personal preferences are at the root of current levels of VOSS, argues that

> ... there is no direct causal link between economic and social development and occupational segregation, or the pay gap; modern and egalitarian societies do not necessarily have lower scores on these two indicators of gender equality in the workforce. The country with the lowest level of occupational segregation in the world is China, not Sweden, as so many believe. Many countries in the Far East have lower levels of occupational segregation than in western Europe. The lowest pay gap in the world is not found in Sweden, as so many claim, but in Swaziland where women earn more than men, on average, followed closely by Sri Lanka.... (Hakim, forthcoming: 2007)

Later, however, Hakim does seem to suggest that there is a causal link between "economic and social development and occupational segregation" but that it is an inversion of what we might expect: "even more disconcerting is the evidence that family-friendly policies generally *reduce* gender equality in the workforce, rather than raising it, as everyone has assumed until now" (Hakim, forthcoming: 2007).

Hakim's contradictory statements on this issue provides further evidence of confusion over the concept of occupational sex segregation. Reference to occupational segregation and the pay gap as two distinct entities leaves unclear what type of segregation, on Hakim's view, is most prevalent in either China or Sweden. Certainly, Sweden does have relatively high levels of segregation but predominantly horizontal segregation (see Blackburn et al, 1999b). Therefore the pay gap is small, in comparison to other European countries, despite substantial levels of overall occupational sex segregation. Hakim's arguments regarding the cross-national comparisons of pay gaps are valid in one sense; a measurement of VOSS (the comparisons of the disproportionate distribution of men and women across occupations according to a vertical ordinal scale of pay) could provide quantitative results showing lower levels of VOSS in Swaziland than in Sweden. However, even if we assume that the data were weighted correctly to allow for direct comparison, we cannot conclude that these results obtain because Sweden has more family-friendly policies than Swaziland. The comparison is misleading as the two economies are not comparable in terms of labour market mechanisms, standards of living, cultural codifications and domestic policies.

In situations where data are comparable, we can in fact detect correlations between levels of VOSS and particular domestic policies. As discussed earlier, paid parental leave in Sweden is proving an increasingly attractive policy to men in a setting in which female activity rates are high and levels of VOSS low. Thus, it may be suggested that in addition to a strong correlation between the rates of paid leave and male take-up rates, there is also a relationship between women's higher earning power and male take-up rates of paid parental leave (Blackburn et al, 1999b). Finally, Hakim seems to overlook how women's choices and preferences may well increase in the presence of increased policy provisions. We should not assume, in the absence of those further options, that all reasonable preferences are already fulfilled.

In arguments that resemble Hakim's, Dermott (2000) has somewhat unpersuasively maintained that the impact of paid parental leave in Sweden is yet to deliver substantial social change. However, even if Dermott were correct, it must be remembered that paid parental leave was only introduced in Sweden in 1974. It has therefore only been available to two generations of fathers. Considering the radical cultural implications of such a scheme in which men's active parenting role is actively recognised and encouraged, two generations is too brief a period on the basis of which to judge its impact on society. One only has to look at the legal reforms to women's rights over the past few decades (examples of which are set out in Appendix 1) to see how ludicrous many of the past limitations on women appear to us today.

Notes

[1] However, it might be of interest to the reader to mention the resurgence of literature over the course of the mid- to late 1990s that argues that in fact stereotypes should be considered as indicators of social reality. See, for example, Judd and Park (1993); Lee et al (1995); Valian (1998); Beyer (1999).

[2] Assumptions about men and women appear throughout society, but I have used the term 'managers' to highlight that, in this context, the views are held by those with decision-making power in the labour market. The same argument might be directed at 'employers', to further illustrate the point.

[3] All EU member states are bound by Article 141 (formerly 119) of the European Community, which stipulates that "each Member State shall ensure that the principle of equal pay for male and female workers for equal work or work of equal value is applied". This directly applicable provision has been supplemented by directives on pay, employment and vocational training, and statutory social security, self-employment and the burden of proof. UK law frequently has had to be amended so as to comply with EU law and with ECJ interpretations of EU law. Thus the previous ETD (76/207/EEC) was amended in 2002 and is relabelled as 2002/73/EC, and now also covers pay discrimination in addition to selection criteria, recruitment, promotion and training, working conditions and dismissals and brings sex discrimination law in line with that relating to 'race', religion or belief, sexual orientation and disability. See Equal Opportunities Review (2002) for detailed discussion of the implications relating to the amended directive.

[4] As amended 2005.

[5] Forty-six per cent of the workers in the British labour market are women and 44% of these work part time (EOC, 2005, p 1).

[6] Although the EqPA was ratified in 1970, it was not implemented until 1975, primarily in order "to give employers time to adjust" (Deakin and Morris, 1998, p 546).

[7] The term 'same employer review' stretches to 'single source', that is, the same employer irrespective of out-sourcing, etc. See *AG Lawrence and Others v Regent Office Care Ltd, Commercial Catering Group and Mitie Secure Services Ltd (Case C-320/00)*.

[8] Since 6 April 2003 individuals who believe that they may not have received equal pay are allowed to request information from their employers (see *Equal Opportunities Review* 117, May 2003, pp13, 22). Previously one had to initiate tribunal proceedings to get the employer to disclose pay data by way of discovery. However, under the new procedure the employer *is allowed to rely on confidentiality* as a ground for refusing to disclose. The new procedure is mainly intended to avoid unnecessary proceedings by allowing women to see whether there is a likely comparator. However, it does not avoid the need for mandatory pay audits that would compel the employer to initiate change. What remains to be seen is whether applicants will be able to use the new ETD wording (2002/73/EC) to tackle pay discrimination that falls outside the scope of Article 141. That is, it is not yet clear whether it will allow claims using a hypothetical comparator rather than, as required by Article 141, an actual comparator. This is a problem exacerbated by high levels of horizontal segregation, whereby the majority of women tend to work in female-dominated occupations. Indeed, according to Grimshaw and Rubery (2001), more than 60% of women's employment is concentrated into 10 occupations.

[9] See note 8.

[10] Claims can be brought at any time during employment and within six months of leaving employment. As a result of the ECJ ruling on the *Preston v Wolverhampton Healthcare NHS Trust litigation (Case C-78/98)*, the 1970 EqPA (Amendment) 2003 Regulations make it clear that, where there was a 'stable' employment relationship between the woman and her employer, the relevant limitation date for bringing an equal pay claim is six months after the end of the stable relationship. There are exceptions, such as when the woman "is under a disability" or where the employer has deliberately concealed a relevant fact, in which case the six-month period will run from the date she discovered or could reasonably have discovered the fact. Also note that the 2003 Regulations limit the back pay that can be claimed, to six years in England and Wales and five years in Scotland (corresponding to the limits in each country for bringing contractual claims).

[11] Article 3(1) of the amended Directive applies to "employment and working conditions, including dismissals, as well as pay, as provided for in the Directive 75/117/EEC", which is the EPD. The EPD requires "the elimination of all discrimination on grounds of sex with regard to all aspects and conditions of remuneration" for the same work or for the work of equal value.

---

[12] *Health & Safety Executive v Cadman* (IRS Employment Review, 2004a, pp 61–3).

[13] Lord Denning, House of Lords Debate (HL Deb), vol 445, cols 901–902, 5 December 1983.

[14] As amended 2005.

[15] Note that under Section 7B of the 1970 EqPA the complainant has the right to ask his or her employer for information that would help to establish whether or not he or she had received equal pay for equal work in comparison to a worker of the opposite sex, and if not what the reasons are for this. See Employment Relations, Employment Act (2002), 'Equal Pay Questionnaire' (www.dti.gov.uk, as of 21 November 2005). In equal pay cases, once a difference in pay is shown between women and men doing work of equal value, the employer has to prove that the difference is genuinely due to 'material factors'. However, just how obligatory these questionnaires actually are and how effectively they are employed is debatable. See, for example, the case of *Sinclair Roche and Temperley and Ors v Heard and anor* (2004) IRLR 76, EAT.

[16] Mothers have the right not to be refused paid leave on the grounds of keeping an appointment for antenatal care according to the 1996 Employment Rights Act, section 99. This specific right is not further considered here.

[17] Unless the woman works in a factory, in which case compulsory maternity leave is four weeks. See the Tailored Interactive Guidance on Employment Rights (www.tiger.gov.uk).

[18] Those eligible for additional leave paid at £100 (or 90% of earnings for the full 26 weeks if this is less than £106 a week) must have completed 26 weeks continuous service with their employer by the beginning of the 14th week before the expected week of childbirth. Additional maternity leave starts immediately after ordinary maternity leave and continues for a further 26 weeks (unpaid).

[19] Or 90% of earnings if less than £106. Fathers are entitled to paternity leave so long as they have been continuously employed with their employer for 26 weeks (ending the 15th week before the baby is due).

[20] Following Britain's eventual acceptance of the EU Social Chapter in 1999, after having rejected the directive in 1994. The right to parental leave has been implemented in Britain under the 1999 Employment Rights Act.

[21] The directive advises that parents should be offered leave up to their child's *eighth* birthday, but included a clause allowing member states to adjust the length of provision.

[22] Note that in the 1980s Britain became the only member state in Europe to have *decreased* maternity rights.

[23] This relates to western European and the US context. See Hobson and Morgan (2002) and the Introduction to this book.

[24] As Ewing argues: "If the law is to contribute to a genuine improvement of the position of women with children, it is crucial to ensure that parenting rights are extended to both parents" (Ewing, 1996, p 154).

[25] In addition to incorporating contemporary sociological and psychological research in her work, Burgess draws from a large array of anthropological research stretching over many decades, ranging from classic studies, such as Malinowski (1927) and Mead (1935), through to more contemporary works such as Hewlett (1991).

[26] There is also a pledge to extend maternity leave (paid at standard rate, currently £106 per week) to one year (Labour Party, 2005, ch 6).

[27] If the father, who has taken transferred leave, subsequently decides to return to work earlier than planned, the untaken leave is automatically lost to the family as a whole.

[28] See National Pensioners Convention (www.npcuk.org) for full discussion.

[29] Current Swedish legislation provides the right to seven weeks paid maternity leave prior to the birth and seven weeks after the birth for all women regardless of employment history. Both sexes are entitled to 480 days (approximately 13 months) leave up until the child's eighth birthday, if they have six months employment history or 12 months over the previous two years. This is shared between the mother and the father, who can choose who will take the leave and when it will be taken. There

are, however, 60 days that are tied specifically to each parent, that is, 30 days each known as 'mamma month' and 'pappa month'. These distinct periods of leave are provided to encourage fathers to take leave. In a similar vein, in Norway every set of parents are entitled to 52 weeks of parental leave at 80% of their earnings or 42 weeks of leave at 100% of their earnings. Up to 39 weeks of leave (at 80% of earnings) or 29 weeks leave (at 100% of earnings) can be taken flexibly as reduced working hours. Where parental leave is taken in the form of reduced hours, the length of leave is extended correspondingly. Four weeks of the parental leave must be taken by the father, otherwise it will be lost.

[30] The high fertility rates in Ireland are likely to be related to lower usage of contraception rather than generous state benefits.

[31] This government scheme offers five lots of 2.5 hours of free childcare per week for 33 weeks a year by registered childcare providers (see 'About us, ten-year strategy, SureStart' at www. surestart.gov.uk/, 21 November 2005).

[32] For this and further references see Daycare Trust (2005a).

[33] In addition to the crèche facilities, other forms of childcare are similarly expensive. For example, the average cost of placing a child (under the age of two) with a full-time childminder is £127 a week, which amounts to over £6,600 a year. Nannies can cost anything from £150 to £400 a week plus tax and national insurance (Daycare Trust, 2005a).

[34] Neither of these tax credit systems affect the universal child benefit, currently paid at £16.50 a week for the eldest child and £11.05 each week for subsequent children. These are benefits for children up to the age of 16 (or up to 18 if in full-time education). Neither do the tax credit systems affect the new government initiative, the Child Trust Fund, introduced in April 2005. This is a universal and progressive savings fund introduced for all children born after 1 September 2002, which includes an initial payment of £250 (up to £500 for low-income families with household income at or below the full Child Tax Credit income threshold). See HM Treasury (2005).

[35] Although the higher the income, the lower the level of benefit.

[36] Due to rise to 80% from April 2006. See HM Treasury (2004).

[37] The 1997 Labour Party Manifesto emphasised that helping lone parents into paid employment was the best way of reducing the poverty prevalent among them. This campaign offered a range of services and advised lone parents on such matters as how to claim the various relevant tax credit systems. These were linked to the National Child Care Strategy, particularly the Sure Start programmes. In 2000, the Treasury declared that its target was to have 70% of lone parents into paid employment by 2010. For a full discussion of these developments, see Millar and Ridge (2002).

[38] The Cadbury Report is officially named 'The Financial Aspects of Corporate Governance' published in 1992 by The Committee on the Financial Aspects of Corporate Governance and Gee and Co. Ltd.

[39] The Turnbull Report is formally entitled 'Internal Control: Guidance for Directors on the Combined Code' published in 1999 by the Institute of Chartered Accountants in England and Wales.

[40] *The Company Law Review* (2001) London: Department of Transport and Industry.

[41] Moreover, although the proportion of organisations that had completed an EPR increased from 15% in 2003 to 21% in 2004, the proportion with their first EPR planned fell from 15% to 9% See Schäfer et al (2004) and also Neathey et al (2004).

FIVE

The seduction of outcomes: concluding remarks

A central theme of this book has been the meaning of outcomes. In analyses of sex segregation *observation* of particular outcomes has all too often been readily assumed to be indicative of particular *causes*. The stubborn survival of VOSS has prompted a range of explanations. Those which proceed from a binary understanding of male and female psychological and/or physiological attributes (Steven Goldberg's Male Dominance Theory, Simon Baron-Cohen's new Empathising/ Systemising Theory and also Carol Gilligan's Different Voice thesis) all assume that the differential behavioural patterns of men and women display a certain predictable fixity. In response, society should accept and facilitate what is an expected dichotomy of outcome without concerning itself too much with attempts to engineer legal and political systems that promote (or indeed enforce) convergence in the patterns of the social behaviour of the two sexes. Those who argue, meanwhile, that the primary causality of VOSS is forms of patriarchy (Sylvia Walby and Valerie Bryson), assume that because men are to be found in greater numbers in positions of power, authority and status, relations between men and women are at root exploitative. Only victory in a clash of interests would lead to the emancipation of women. Finally, human capital-based accounts of VOSS in terms of the distribution and deployment of human capital (Becker's Rational Choice Theory, Hakim's Preference Theory) bounce repeatedly between observation and perceived cause. These are perhaps the most circular of all the arguments in the sense that women are perceived to be worthy of lower wages and status because they occupy lower wages and status – an imputed consequence of their lifestyle choices and preferences. The conditions in which men and women make these choices are not considered restrictive enough to challenge predicted drives to fulfil stereotypical social roles; the employer is infrequently judged anything less than a dependable mediator of economic worth. Consequently, in this account, in an era when 'choice is available to all', policies set forth to combat unequal outcomes between the sexes are merely unwarranted interference in the efficient workings of the labour market.

VOSS is, in and of itself, nothing more or less than an unequal outcome. Its occurrence should not be automatically interpreted as a site of injustice. Yet neither should it be automatically interpreted as reflecting the characteristics of men and women or their respective preferences.

Occupational sex segregation (overall segregation) is the resultant of a complex relationship between its two constitutive dimensions, vertical and horizontal. It is only possible to identify VOSS as the manifestation of injustice, when its causes are confirmed as the result of malpractice or unreasonably restricted opportunities. Discerning what these might constitute is a matter first of normative deliberation and consequently of the interpretation of accepted social and political objectives.

Central to any account of equality is the normative principle of equal treatment (Habermas, 1983; Kymlicka, 1990; Nagel, 1991), which is understood as prescribing treatment of individuals as equals, that is, with equal concern and respect (Dworkin, 1977, p 370). It emphatically does not maintain that all individuals are indistinguishable and thus should be treated uniformly. To treat people *equally*, in this latter sense, might of course be appropriate according to the principle of equal treatment but is not necessarily so. This subtlety allows the creation of institutions and structures that can constructively and justly administer the equal treatment of individuals who are alike in 'relevant respects'. As we have seen in detail throughout the last chapter, such is the principle on which the EU has construed its particular 'Equal Treatment Principle' (ETP), now the bedrock of Britain's equality and anti-discrimination laws. Under the ETP, central to the decision as to whether certain lifestyle restrictions leading to VOSS are related to injustice, is the specific interpretation of the 'relevant respects' in which individuals should be treated equally.

Using empirical examples this study has illustrated how many institutional and policy-based restrictions on lifestyle options available to individuals are based on stereotypical assumptions about the capabilities of each sex, irrespective of normative and practical ambitions. A major feature of these lifestyle restrictions has been the issue of work–life balance. In describing the need to widen practical lifestyle options, the aim has been not to prescribe how men and women, or each as parents, *should* act but rather to show how the opportunity to fulfil various aspirations, preferences or needs is inhibited by the curtailment of choice. Such curtailment is principally and systematically generated by the misguided and widespread social and institutional assumptions that one sex necessarily commands superior parenting abilities. The majority of funded provisions for supporting the role of parents are available *only* to women, which leads to 'systemic dissonance' between the actual aspirations/preferences of female and male workers alike and the structured environment in which their work–life balance choices are to be made. This inability to fulfil certain preferences, the resulting restrictions and the perpetuation of social norms consequent on them, lead to substantive inequality between men and women. Accordingly, we should critically interrogate the current assumptions that underpin purportedly sound interpretations of ETP and the stereotypes that they effectively serve to uphold. In so doing, we should attempt to prise apart anti-discrimination measures (leaving aside specific measures designed to protect health) and an inadequately conceived understanding of how women and men differ. Rather than aligning policy provision with the current set of unequal outcomes, we need not only to afford individuals far more freedom to explore and realise their preferences and needs, we must also facilitate the emergence of new social norms and institutional procedures, which better lend themselves to the equal treatment of individuals who are alike in 'relevant respects'. In the absence of a thoroughgoing reinterpretation of what is 'relevant' to both men and women in the 21st century, the current persistance of VOSS, even in an organisation with the innovative and progressive track record of the BBC, will defy satisfactory explanation. It will only be on the basis of an extended sphere of choice available to both sexes that VOSS might ever be finally indentified as a function of natural difference, respective preferences or malpratice. In the meantime, the provision of extended opportunity should be our primary focus.

References

Ahlgren, A. and Johnson, D. (1979) 'Sex differences in cooperative and competitive attitudes from the 2nd through the 12th grades', *Developmental Psychology*, vol 15, pp 45-49 [in S. Baron-Cohen (2003) *The essential difference: Male and female brains and the truth about autism*, New York, NY: Basic Books].

Andelin, H.B. (1965) *Fascinating womanhood*, Maryland, MD: Pacific Press.

Baron-Cohen, S. (2003) *The essential difference: Male and female brains and the truth about autism*, New York, NY: Basic Books.

Baron-Cohen, S. (2005) 'Scientists have sex on the brain', *Guardian Weekly* (www.guardian.co.uk/guardianweekly/story/0,,1404110,00.html), 4 February.

Baron-Cohen, S. (2006) *A political system based on empathy*, Edge, The World Question Center, 'What is your dangerous idea?' (www.edge.org/questioncenter.html).

Baron-Cohen, S. (forthcoming: 2007) 'Does biology play any role in sex differences in the mind?', in J. Browne (ed) *The future of gender*, Cambridge: Cambridge University Press.

Bartlett, K. (1990) 'Feminist Legal Methods', *Harvard Law Review*, vol 103, pp 829-88.

Bartlett, W., Roberts, J. and Le Grand, J. (1998) *A revolution in social policy*, Bristol: The Policy Press.

BBC 'Salary Ranges' 1997/98. (Unpublished)

BBC Annual Report 1997/1998. London: BBC.

BBC Manager's Guidelines: People in Focus. (Unpublished)

BBC Website: www.bbc.co.uk

Beal, C. (1994) *Boys and girls: The development of gender roles*, New York, NY: McGraw-Hill.

Becker, G. (1981/91) *A treatise on the family*, Cambridge, MA: Harvard University Press.

Bell, C. (1983) *Fathers, Childbirth and Work*, Manchester: Equal Opportunities Commission.

Benbow, C. (1988) 'Sex differences in mathematical reasoning ability in intellectually talented preadolescents: their nature, effects, and possible causes', *Behavioral and Brain Sciences*, 11, pp 169-232 [in S. Baron-Cohen (2003) *The essential difference: Male and female brains and the truth about autism*, New York, NY: Basic Books].

Benhabib, S. (1994) 'From identity politics to social feminism: a plea for the nineties' (www.ed.uiuc.edu/eps/PES-Yearbook/94_docs/BENHABIB.htm).

Beutel, A. and Marini, M. (1995) 'Gender and values', *American Sociological Review*, no 60, pp 436-48.

Beyer, S. (1999) 'Gender differences in the accuracy of grade expectations and self-evaluations', *Sex Roles*, vol 41, p 279.

Blackburn, R. and Mann, M. (1979) *The working class in the labour market*, London: Macmillan.

Blackburn, R., Brooks, B. and Jarman, J. (1999a) 'Gender inequality in the labour market: the vertical dimension of occupational segregation', *Cambridge Studies in Social Research*, no 3, Cambridge: Sociological Research Group, University of Cambridge.

Blackburn, R., Jarman, J. and Brooks, B. (1999b) 'The relation between gender inequality and occupational segregation in 32 countries', *Cambridge Studies in Social Research*, no 2, Cambridge: Sociological Research Group, University of Cambridge.

Blackburn, R., Brooks, B. and Jarman, J. (2001) 'The vertical dimension of occupational segregation', *Work, Employment and Society*, vol 15, no 3, pp 511-38.

Bleier, R. (1984) *Gender and science*, Oxford: Pergamon.

Brewer, M., Goodman, A., Shaw, J. and Shephard, A. (2005) 'Poverty and inequality in Britain 2005', *Commentary*, no 99, London: Institute for Fiscal Studies.

Browne, J. (2004). 'Resolving gender pay inequality? Rationales, enforcement and policy,' *Journal of Social Policy*, vol 33, no 4, pp 553-71.

Browne, J., Deakin, S. and Wilkinson, F. (2005) 'Capabilities, social rights and European market integration', in R. Salais and R. Villeneuve (eds) *Europe and the politics of capabilities*, Cambridge: Cambridge University Press.

Browne, J. (nd) PhD thesis, unpublished, Cambridge: Cambridge University.

Bryson, V. (1992) *Feminist political theory*, London: Macmillan.

Bryson, V. (forthcoming: 2007) 'Perspectives on gender equality: challenging the terms of debate', in J. Browne (ed) *The future of gender*, Cambridge: Cambridge University Press.

Burchell, B. (1996) 'Gender segregation, size of workplace and the public sector', *Gender, Work and Organisation*, vol 3, no 4, pp 227-35.

Burchell, B. and Rubery, J. (1990) 'An empirical investigation into the segmentation of the labour supply', *Work Employment and Society*, vol 4, no 4, pp 551-75.

Burgess, A. (1997) *Fatherhood reclaimed: The making of the modern father*, London: Vermillion.

Burgess, A. and Ruxton, S. (1996) *Men and their children: Proposals for public policy*, London: Institute for Public Policy Research.

Butler, J. (1990) *Gender trouble*, London: Routledge.

Cadbury Committee (1992) *Report of the committee on financial aspects of corporate governance*, London: Gee.

Cahn, N. (1991) 'Defining feminist litigation', *Harvard Women's Law Journal*, no 14, pp 1-20.

Carver, T. (forthcoming: 2007) '"Trans" trouble: trans-sexuality and the end of gender', in J. Browne (ed) *The future of gender*, Cambridge: Cambridge University Press.

Charles, N. (1993) *Gender divisions and social change*, Hemel Hempstead: Harvester Wheatsheaf.

Charles, N. and Kerr, M. (1988) *Women, food and families*, Manchester: Manchester University Press.

Charlesworth, W. and Dzur, C. (1987) 'Gender comparisons of preschoolers' behavior and resource utilization in group problem solving', *Child Development*, 58, pp 191-200 [in S. Baron-Cohen (2003) *The essential difference: Male and female brains and the truth about autism*, New York, NY: Basic Books].

Cockburn, C. (1983) *Brothers: Male dominance and technological change*, London: Pluto Press.

Colman, A. and Colman, L. (1988) *The father: Mythology and changing roles*, Wilmette, IL: Chiron.

Connell, R. (1987) *Gender and power: Society, the person and sexual politics*, Cambridge: Polity Press.

Corti, L. and Dex, S. (1995) 'Highly qualified women', *Employment Gazette*, vol 103, no 3, pp 115-21.

Craig, C., Ruber, J., Tarling, R. and Wilkinson, F. (1982) *Labour market structure, industrial organisation and low pay*, Cambridge: Cambridge University Press.

Cranston, R. (1985) *Legal foundations of the welfare state*, London: Weidenfeld and Nicolson.

Crick, N. and Grotpeter, J. (1995) 'Relational aggression, gender, and social-psychological adjustment', *Child Development*, 66, pp 710-22 [in S. Baron-Cohen (2003) *The essential difference: Male and female brains and the truth about autism*, New York, NY: Basic Books].

Crompton, R. (1997) *Women and work in modern Britain*, Oxford: Oxford University Press.

Crompton, R. (forthcoming: 2007) 'Gender inequality and the gendered division of labour', in J. Browne (ed) *The future of gender*, Cambridge: Cambridge University Press.

Crompton, R. and Harris, F. (1998) 'Explaining women's employment patterns: "orientations to work" revisited', *British Journal of Sociology*, vol 49, no 1, pp 118-36.

Crompton, R. and Sanderson, K. (1990) *Gendered jobs and social change*, London: Unwin Hyman.

Daycare Trust (2001) (www.daycaretrust.org).

Daycare Trust (2005a) 'Childcare facts: about childcare costs', Daycare Trust: The National Childcare Campaign (www.daycaretrust.org, accessed 21 November).

Daycare Trust (2005b) *Childcare for all?*, Progress Report (November 2005), The National Childcare Strategy, London: Daycare Trust.

Daycare Trust (2005c) 'Childcare facts: about poverty', Daycare Trust: The National Childcare Campaign (www.daycaretrust.org, accessed 21 November 2006).

Deakin, S. and Morris, G. (1998) *Labour law*, London: Butterworths.

Delphy, C. (1984) *Close to home: A materialist analysis of women's oppression*, London: Hutchinson.

Dermott, E. (2000) *Parental leave 'new' fatherhood in practice*, Conference Paper. Sociological Research Group Conference, 20th-22nd September 2000. University of Cambridge: Cambridge. (Unpublished)

DfES (Department of Education and Skills) (2002) *Education and training statistics for the United Kingdom, 2002*, London: DfES.

DTI (Department of Trade and Industry) (2005) *Individual incomes 1996-2004*, London: DTI.

Dupré, J. (2001) *Human nature and the limits of science*, Oxford: Oxford University Press.

Dworkin, R. (1977) *Taking rights seriously*, Cambridge: Harvard University Press.

England, P. (1984) 'Wage appreciation and depreciation: a test of neo-classical economic explanations of occupational sex segregation', *Social Forces*, 62, pp 726-49.

EOC (Equal Opportunities Commission) (2003) 'Employers must tackle complacency and secrecy on equal pay', Embargo: 00.1 24 March (www.eoc.org.uk/Default.aspx?page=15167&lang=en).

EOC Annual Report 2003, Manchester: EOC.

EOC (2005) *Facts about men and women in Great Britain*, Manchester: EOC.

Equal Opportunities Review (2002) *Revised equal treatment directive*, EOR No 106, June, pp 22-25.

Equal Opportunities Review (2003) EOR No 117, May, pp 13, 22.

Erhardt, A. and Meyer-Bahlburg, H. (1981) 'Effects of prenatal sex hormones on gender-related behaviour', *Science*, no 211, pp 1312-18.

Ewing, K. (ed) (1996) *Working life: A new perspective on labour law*, London: Lawrence and Wishart.

Fagan, C. and O'Reilly, J. (1998) 'Conceptualising part-time work', in J. O'Reilly and C. Fagan (eds) *Part-time prospects: An international comparison of part-time work in Europe, North America and the Pacific Rim*, London: Routledge, pp 1-32.

Fagan, C. and Rubery, J. (1996) 'The salience of the part-time divide in the European Union', *European Sociological Review*, December, no 12, pp 227-50.

Faludi, S. (1992) *Backlash: The undeclared war against women*, London: Chatto & Windus.

Felstead, A., Ashton, D. and Green, F. (2000) 'Are Britain's workplace skills becoming more unequal?', *Cambridge Journal of Economics*, vol 24, no 6, pp 709-27.

Fredman, S. (1997) *Women and the law*, Oxford: Oxford University Press.

Friedl, E. (1975) *Women and men: An anthropologist's view*, New York, NY: Holt Reinhart and Winston.

Geary, D. (1996) 'Sexual selection and sex differences in mathematical abilities', *Behavioral and Brain Sciences*, 19, pp 229-84 [in S. Baron-Cohen (2003) *The essential difference: Male and female brains and the truth about autism*, New York, NY: Basic Books].

Geary, D. (1998) *Male, female: The evolution of human sex differences*, Washington, DC: American Psychological Association [in Baron-Cohen, S. (forthcoming 2007) 'Does biology play any role in sex differences in the mind?', in J. Browne (ed) *The future of gender*, Cambridge: Cambridge University Press].

Gilligan, C. (1981, 1993) *In a different voice: Psychological theory and women's development*, Cambridge, MA: Harvard University Press.

Gilligan, C. (1982/93) *In a different voice: Psychological theory and women's development*, Cambridge, MA: Harvard University Press.

Gilligan, C. (1987) 'Gender difference and morality', in E. Kittay and D. Meyers (eds) *Women and moral theory*, Savage, MD: Rowman and Littlefield, pp 19-33.

Goldberg, S. (1979) *The inevitability of patriarchy*, New York, NY: William Morrow.

Goldberg, S. (1993) *Why men rule: The theory of male dominance*, Chicago, IL: Open Court.

Goldstein, J. (2001) *War and gender: How gender shames the war system and visa versa*, Cambridge: Cambridge University Press.

Goldthorpe, J., Lockwood, D., Bechhofer, F. and Platt, J. (1968) *The affluent worker: Industrial attitudes and behaviour*, Cambridge: Cambridge University Press.

Greer, G. (1999) *The whole woman*, London: Anchor.

Gregg, P. and Washbrook, E. (2003) *The effects of early maternal employment on understanding the impact of poverty on children of the 90s*, CMPO Working Paper Series no 03/070, Bristol: The Centre for Market and Public Organisation.

Grimshaw, D. and Rubery, J. (2001) *The gender pay gap: A research review*, EOC Research Discussion Series, Manchester: EOC.

Haas, L. and Hwang, C.P. (2005) 'The impact of taking parental leave on fathers' participation in childcare and ties with children: lessons from Sweden', Conference Paper, First International Conference: 'Community, Work and Family', 16-18 March, Manchester (see www.did.stu.mmu.ac.uk/cwf/Haas_HwangManchester.doc).

Habermas, J. (1983) 'Discourse ethics: notes on a program of philosophical justification', in J. Habermas, *Moral consciousness and communicative action*, tr. C. Lenhardt and S. Weber Nicholsen (1990) Cambridge, MA: MIT Press.

Hakim, C. (1996) *Key issues in women's work: Female heterogeneity and the polarisation of women's employment*, London: Athlone.

Hakim, C. (1998) 'Developing a sociology for the twenty-first century: preference theory', *British Journal of Sociology*, vol 49, no 1, pp 138-43.

Hakim, C. (1999) 'Models of the family, women's role and social policy: a new perspective from preference theory', *European Societies*, April, vol 1, no 1, pp 25-50.

Hakim (forthcoming: 2007) 'The politics of female diversity in the 21st century', in J. Browne (ed) *The future of gender*, Cambridge: Cambridge University Press.

Hartmann, H. (1982) 'Capitalism, patriarchy and job segregation by sex', reprinted in A. Giddens and D. Held (eds) *Classes, power and conflict*, London: Macmillan, pp 446-69.

Hatter, W., Vinter, L. and Williams, R. (2002) *Dads on dads: Needs and expectations at home and at work*, Manchester: EOC.

Hepple, B. (1984) *Equal pay and the industrial tribunals*, London: Sweet and Maxwell.

Hepple, B. (1995) 'Social values and European law', vol 48, issue 2, *Current Legal Problems*, pp 39-61.

Hepple, B (2002) 'Enforcement: the law and politics of cooperation and compliance', in B.Hepple (ed) *Social and labour rights in a global context: International and comparative perspectives*, Cambridge: Cambridge University Press.

Hewlett, B. (1991) *Intimate fathers: the nature and content of paternal infant care*, Ann Arbor, MI: University of Michigan Press.

HM Treasury (2004) 'Choice for parents, the best start for children: a ten year strategy for childcare', December (at www.hm-treasury.gov.uk, accessed 21 November 2005) p 1.

HM Treasury (2005) 'Savings, Child Trust Fund' (at www.hm-treasury.gov.uk, accessed 21 November).

Hobson, B. and Morgan, D. (2002) 'Introduction: making men into fathers', in B. Hobson (ed) *Making men into fathers: Men, masculinities and the social politics of fatherhood*, Cambridge: Cambridge University Press, p 1-21.

ICM Research Survey (1996) 'Genderquake Survey' (conducted for the Barass Company, April 1996), in S. Franks (1999) *Having none of it: Men, women and the future of work*, London: Granta Books.

IRS Employment Review (2004a) Issue 804, July 2004. IRS. See http://www.irser.co.uk/

IRS Employment Review (2004b) Issue 798, April 2004 IRS. See http://www.irser.co.uk/

Jarman, J. (1992) *Which way forward? Conceptual issues from the current proposals to amend the British Equal Pay Act*, Sociological Research Group Working Papers, no 8, Cambridge: Cambridge University Press.

Jenkins, R., Pearson, R. and Seyfang, G. (2002) *Corporate responsibility and labour rights*, London: Earthscan.

Jennings, K. (1977) 'People versus object orientation in preschool children: do sex differences really occur?', *Journal of Genetic Psychology*, 131, pp 65-73 [in S. Baron-Cohen (2003) *The essential difference: Male and female brains and the truth about autism*, New York, NY: Basic Books].

Joshi, H. and Paci, P. (1998) *Unequal pay for women and men: Evidence from the British birth cohort studies*, Cambridge, MA: MIT Press.

Judd, C.M. and Park, B. (1993) 'Definition and assessment of accuracy in social stereotypes', *Psychology Review*, 100, pp 109-28.

Kingsmill, D. (2001) *Review of women's employment and pay*, London: DTI.

Knight, G. and Chao, C.-C. (1989) 'Gender differences in the cooperative, competitive, and individualistic social values of children', *Motivation and Emotion*, 13, pp 125-41 [in S. Baron-Cohen (2003) *The essential difference: Male and female brains and the truth about autism*, New York, NY: Basic Books].

Kymlicka, W. (1990) *Contemporary Political Philosophy*, Oxford: Clarendon Press.

Labour Party (2005) *Labour Party Manifesto*, London: Labour Party.

Lee, Y.-T., Jussim, L. and McCauley, C. (1995) *Stereotype accuracy: Toward appreciating group differences*, Washington, DC: APA Books.

Lewis, J. (2002) 'The problem of fathers: policy and behaviour in Britain', in B. Hobson and D. Morgan (eds) *Making men into fathers: Men, masculinities and the social politics of fatherhood*, Cambridge: Cambridge University Press, pp 125-49.

Lowe, M. and Hubbard, R. (eds) (1983) *Woman's nature: Rationalisation of inequality*, Oxford: Pergamon.

MacKinnon, C. (1983) 'Feminism, Marxism, method and the state: toward feminist jurisprudence', *Signs: Journal of Women in Culture and Society*, 635, p 8.

MacKinnon, C. (1987) 'Feminism, Marxism, Method and the state: an agenda for theory', *Signs: Journal of Women in Culture and Society*, 7, pp 515-44.

Maclean, M. (1991) *Surviving divorce*, London: Macmillan.

Malinowski, B. (1927) 'The father in primitive psychology', New York, NY: Norton.

Marshall, T. and Bottomore, T. (1992) *Citizenship and social class*, London: Pluto Perspectives.

Mead, M. (1935) 'Sex and temperament in 3 primitive societies', New York, NY: Morrow.

Meehan, E. (1985) *Rights at work: Campaigns and policy in Britain and the United States*, Macmillan: Basingstoke.

Menkel-Meadow, C. (1987) 'Portia in a different voice: speculating on a women's lawyering process', *Berkeley Women's Law Journal*, 1, pp 39-63.

Millar, J. and Ridge, T. (2002) 'Parents, children, families and New Labour: developing family policy?', in M. Powel (ed) *Evaluating New Labour's welfare reforms*, Bristol: The Policy Press.

Mincer, J. (1966) 'Labour force participation and unemployment: a review of recent evidence', in R. Gordon and M. Gordon (eds) *Prosperity and unemployment*, New York, NY: Wiley, pp 73-134.

Mitchell, J., and Oakley, A. (1976) (eds) *The rights and wrongs of women*, London. Penguin Books.

Moss, P., Holtermann, S., Owen, C. and Brannen, J. (1999) 'Lone parents and the labour market revisited', in *Labour Market Trends, November,* London: Office for National Statistics, pp 583-94.

Nagel, T. (1991) *Equality and Partiality,* Oxford: Oxford University Press.

National Council of Women (1992) 'Superwoman keeps going: understanding the female web, a survey of women's lives and expectations', in S. Franks (1999) *Having none of it: Men, women and the future of work,* London: Granta Books, p 14.

Neathey, F., Dench, S. and Thomson, L. (2003) *Monitoring progress towards pay equality,* EOC Research Discussion Series, Manchester: EOC, March.

Neathey, F., Willison, R., Akroyd, K., Regan, J. and Hill, D. (2004) *Equal pay reviews in practice,* Manchester: EOC.

Nussbaum, M. (2000) *Women and human development,* Cambridge: Cambridge University Press.

Oakley, A. (1972) *Sex, gender and society,* London: Temple Smith.

O'Brien, M. and Shemilt, I. (2003) *Working fathers: Earning and caring,* EOC Research and Discussion Series, Manchester: EOC.

Ogus, A., Barendt, E. and Wikeley, N. (1995) *The law of social security,* London: Butterworths.

ONS (2005a) *The demographic characteristics of the oldest old in the United Kingdom,* Population Trends 120, Summer, London: ONS.

ONS (2005b) 'Labour market, more lone parents working' (www.statistics.gov.uk, accessed 21 November).

Pahl, J. (1989) *Money and marriage,* Basingstoke: Macmillan.

Parsons, T. (1942) 'Age and sex in the social structure of the United States', *American Sociological Review,* 7, pp 604-16.

Pilcher, J. (1999) *Women in contemporary Britain: An introduction,* London: Routledge.

Pinker, S. and Spelke, E.S. (2005) *The science of gender and science: Pinker vs Spelke: A debate,* Harvard University, Mind/Brain/Behaviour Initiative (www.edge.org/documents/archive/edge160.html#d).

Pittmann, F. (1993) 'Man enough: fathers, sons and the search for masculinity', New York, NY: Berkeley Publishing Co.

Polacheck, S. (1981) 'Occupational self-selection: a human capital approach to sex differences in occupational structure', *Review of Economics and Statistics,* February, pp 60-9.

Polan, D. (1982) 'Toward a theory of law and Patriarchy', in David Kairys (ed) *The politics of law: A progressive critique,* New York, NY: Pantheon Books.

Pollert, A. (1996) '"Gender and class revisited", or "The poverty of patriarchy"', *Sociology*, vol 30, no 4, pp 639-59.

Posner, R. (1992) *Economic analysis of law*, (4th edn) London: Little, Brown and Company.

Power, T.G. (1985) 'Mother- and father-infant play: a developmental analysis', in S. Baron-Cohen (2003) *The essential difference: Male and female brains and the truth about autism*, New York, NY: Basic Books.

Prandy, K., Stewart, A. and Blackburn, R. (1983) *White collar unionism*, London: Macmillan.

Rifkin, J. (1980) 'Toward a theory of law and patriarchy' *Harvard Women's Law Journal*, 3, pp 89-95.

Rose, S. (1987) *Molecules and minds*, Milton Keynes: Open University Press.

Rosenberg, R. (1982) *Beyond separate spheres: Intellectual roots of modern feminism*, New Haven, CT: Yale University Press.

Rubenstein, M. (1984) *Equal pay for work of equal value*, London: Macmillan.

Rubenstein, M. (2004) 'Equal value procedures to be improved', *Equal Opportunities Review*, no 121, July.

Rubenstein, M. (2005) 'Amending the Sex Discrimination Act', *Equal Opportunities Review*, no 140, April.

Rubery, J., Horrell, S. and Burchell, B. (1994) 'Part-time work and gender inequality in the labour market', in A. MacEwen Scott (ed) *Gender segregation and social change*, Oxford: Oxford University Press, pp 205-34.

Sayers, J. (1982) *Biological politics*, London: Tavistock.

Schäfer, S., Winterbotham, M., and McAndrew, F. (2004) *Equal Pay reviews survey 2004*, Manchester: EOC.

Shorter, E. (1976) 'Women's work: what difference did capitalism make?', *Theory and Society*, 3, pp 513-27.

Smith, P.M. (1985) *Language, the sexes and society*, Oxford: Blackwell.

Strayer, F. (1980) 'Child ethology and the study of preschool social relations', in H. Foot, A. Chapman and J. Smith (eds) *Friendship and social relations in children*, Chichester: John Wiley & Sons [in S. Baron-Cohen (2003) *The essential difference: Male and female brains and the truth about autism*, New York, NY: Basic Books].

Summers, L.H. (2005) Speech at the National Bureau of Economic Research Conference 'Diversifying the Science and Engineering Workforce', Cambridge, MA, 14 January (www.president.harvard.edu/speeches/2005/nber.html).

Sunstein, C. (1997) *Free markets and social justice*, New York, NY: Oxford University Press.

Tavris, C. (1992) *The mismeasure of woman*, New York, NY: Simon and Schuster.

Taylor, J., Gilligan, C. and Sullivan, A. (1995) *Between voice and silence: Women and girls, race and relationship*, Cambridge, MA: Harvard University Press.

Thornton, M. (1986) 'Feminist jurisprudence: illusion or reality?' *Australian Journal of Law and Society*, 3, pp 5-29.

Tong, R. (1997) *Feminist thought: A comprehensive introduction*, London: Routledge.

Treadwell, P. (1987) 'Biologic influences on masculinity', in H. Brod (ed) *The making of masculinities*, London: Allen & Unwin, pp 259-85.

Treanor, J. (2001) 'Waging war on sex bias', *The Guardian*, 6 December.

Treiman, D. and Hartmann, H. (eds) (1981) *Women, work and wages: Equal pay for jobs of equal value*, Washington DC, National Academic Press.

Turnbull Report (1999) www.frc.org.uk/corporate/internalcontrol.cfm

Valian, V. (1998) *Why so slow? The advancement of women*, Cambridge, MA: MIT.

Walby, S. (1986) *Patriarchy at work*, Cambridge: Polity Press.

Walby, S. (1990) *Theorising patriarchy*, Oxford: Blackwell.

Walby, S. (1997) *Gender transformations*, London: Routledge.

Waldfogel, J. (1993) *Women working for less: A longitudinal analysis of the family gap*, Welfare State Working Paper, 93, London: STICERD, London School of Economics and Political Science.

Waldfogel, J. (1995) 'The price of motherhood: family status and women's pay in a young British cohort', *Oxford Economic Papers*, 47, pp 584-610.

Wark, G. and Krebs, D. (1996) 'Gender and dilemma differences in real-life moral judgement', *Developmental Psychology*, 32, pp 220-30.

White, S. (ed) (2001) *New labour: The progressive future?*, Basingstoke: Palgrave.

Wilson, E.O. (1975/82) *Sociobiology: The new synthesis*, Cambridge, MA: Harvard University Press.

Women and Equality Unit (2006) Tackling Occupational Segregation Fact Sheet: Women's Economic Participation Team 31 March 2006. London: WEU. Also see: www.womenandequalityunit.gov.uk/publications/tackling_occupseg_facts_apr06.pdf

ONS data

Census, April 2001.

Household and Family Data, 2001.

Labour Force Survey, Spring 2002.
Labour Force Survey, Spring 2003.
Labour Market Trends, November 2003.
Labour Force Survey, Spring 2004.
Quarterly Labour Force Survey, December 2004–February 2005.
Annual Survey of Hours and Earnings.2005.

Appendix 1: Examples of important reforms to British law relevant to sex equality[1]

1918   Women aged 30 or over are given the right to vote in general elections.

1919   *Sex Disqualification (Removal) Act (1919)* technically opened positions to women in civil or judicial office and jury service. However, this Act was known as a 'dead letter' as it was severely restricted by a wide range of exclusionary regulations such as marriage bars and admissions regulations based on educational qualifications, which most women were unable to attain (for example, many universities were not required to make provision for the admission of women to certain courses such as medicine and law).

1923   *Matrimonial Causes Act (1923)*. Under this Act, women were finally granted the right to divorce on the grounds of adultery (previously this right had only been granted to men).

1928   Women over 21 years of age were given the right to vote (the same legal voting age of men).

1939-45 Second World War. Due to the absence of large numbers of men at war, most single women (aged between 20 and 30) were conscripted into the labour market under a policy introduced in 1941. By 1943, 90% of single women and 80% of married women between the ages of 18 and 40 worked in industry or the armed forces[2]. State-run nurseries were provided for children of working mothers[3] and also 'British Restaurants' were set up to provide wholesome and cheap meals, thus alleviating women's domestic duties at home. However, women were not granted the same pay as men were (or had been) in the same jobs.

1942   Beveridge Report was introduced and served to outline the Welfare State benefit system.

1944   *Education Act (1944).* The duty to provide secondary education for all children up to the age of 15 was established in the Education Act, thus ensuring a minimum standard of education for all females and males[4]. Additionally, this Act formally ended the marriage bar to female teachers[5].

1946   Abolition of the marriage bar. Although informally wavered during the Second World War, the marriage bar was formally lifted from many government services (for example the Civil Service) in 1946[6]. This set a general precedent within the British market, although marriage bars were not formally outlawed in all sectors of the labour market until 1975 (see 1975 Sex Discrimination Act).

1955   Equal pay was introduced in government services such as the Civil Service and schools (although the policy was phased in over a seven-year period). Within the private sector, however, different pay scales for men and women remained until 1975; see 1970 Equal Pay Act.

1961   First birth control pill goes on sale. Free contraceptive supplies under the National Health Service (NHS) were not introduced until 1974.

1967   *Abortion Act* (1967). This Act legalised abortion on medical or psychological grounds.

1969   Wives can enter into financial and legal contracts in their own right.

1970   *Equal Pay Act (1970)* – see 1975.

1973   Britain signs the EC Treaty (Treaty of Rome, 1957). Under this Britain is bound by Article 141 (formerly 119), which stipulates that "each Member State shall ensure that the principle of equal pay for male and female workers for equal work or work of equal value is applied". This Article, later to be built on by subsequent treaties, is the cornerstone of equal pay legislation in the EU.

1975   The right to paid maternity leave for working women is introduced[7]. This was funded by a Maternity Pay Fund to which employers were required to contribute and from which they could claim a full rebate[8]. Also the *1975 Employment Protection Act* was introduced, which gave female employees the right to return to work after maternity leave. Thus, it became automatically unfair to dismiss an employee on grounds of pregnancy.

Sex Discrimination Act (1975) makes sex discrimination unlawful in employment. This Act states that it is illegal to treat one sex less favourably than the other (or married people less favourably than single people) in education, training and employment or in the provision of goods, facilities or services. Furthermore the issue of indirect discrimination was recognised and has been made illegal (discussed in Chapter Four).

Equal Pay Act (1970) comes into force, stating that it is illegal to discriminate between women and men in terms of rates of pay. It specifies that women and men are entitled to the same pay if doing the same type of work (discussed in Chapter Four).

Equal Opportunities Commission was set up. This Commission is a statutory body that has the power to assist individuals and institutions in cases of discrimination. It is able to conduct a formal investigation into cases of discriminatory practices.

1988   *Financial Act (1988)* (which came into effect in 1990). Under this Act, each spouse is responsible for paying tax on his or her own income. As a result, any repayments of tax relating to a wife's income are paid to her and she is able to keep her financial details private.

1991   Until 1991, a husband who forced his wife to have intercourse could not be found guilty of rape, except in limited circumstances. This was not changed through a legislative act but rather a precedent was set in a case of common law in 1991 (*R v R* [1991] 4 All England Reports (All ER) 481).

1999   European Union (EU) Parental Leave Directorate, December 1999. This offers up to three months' unpaid parental leave for the parents of each child (discussed in Chapter Four).

2002   Labour government introduces statutory paternity leave of two weeks, paid at the rate of statutory maternity leave benefit (discussed in Chapter Four).

2006   Labour government propose changes to UK maternity leave provision by which fathers are able to share a proportion of the leave period at the statutory maternity leave benefit rate (discussed in Chapter Four).

Notes

[1] Main source adapted from Fredman's historical account of 'women and the law' (1997). Additional sources are footnoted where applicable.

[2] This period has been noted as a major catalyst to women's rising employment rates over the past five decades. After the Second World War, women, on the one hand, were urged to return home to rebuild the family. The ideology of full-time motherhood and domesticity that had never fully receded was resuscitated with vigour. On the other hand, it was clear that the labour force without women fell substantially short of industry's demand for labour. This prompted the Ministry of Labour in 1947 to appeal to women to enter industry if they were in a position to do so. Thus, the opportunity for married women to enter paid employment on a grand scale was set in place (and for many part-time work was seen as a compromise).

[3] However, government nurseries were inadequate, catering for only about 25% of the children of working mothers and often providing shorter hours than the mothers' working day. Furthermore, at the end of the Second World War, these nurseries were gradually closed, as they had only been considered as an aid to the 'war effort' and not a permanent feature of state-provided services.

[4] Inevitably education has been a key factor in the socialisation of girls and boys. Mitchell and Oakley (1976) illustrate that during the 19th and

early 20th centuries, notions of 'femininity' led to marked differences in the content of girls' and boys' education, resulting in few women being able to compete equally with men within the labour market. Moreover, 'femininity' was intrinsically linked to the upper and middle classes, leading to very different educational experiences for working-class girls (see Mitchell and Oakley, 1976).

[5] The ethos of gender equality within the 1944 Education Act is further illustrated by a clause that offered equal pay for both male and female teachers, which was passed by a majority of one vote in Parliament. However, this clause was reversed when Churchill (Prime Minister 1940-45) called a no-confidence vote (see Cranston, 1985).

[6] The effect of marriage bars in some areas of employment had been hugely detrimental to the progression of women's careers. Not only did women have to leave their jobs on marriage but also employers were reluctant to train or promote women due to the expectation of marriage (and consequent resignation). The result was that very few women reached senior positions.

[7] The earliest maternity benefit (not related to women's employment) had been a small amount exclusively paid to insured workers or their wives for medical care in the National Health Insurance Scheme of 1911. This was overtaken by free healthcare provided by the NHS after the Second World War. In 1946 the National Health Insurance Scheme provided a maternity grant for non-medical costs but it was never intended to cover the whole costs of maternity and thus was a small amount (and during the 1970s the amount was frozen at £25). The provision was cut as a universal entitlement in 1986 and claims for maternity expenses are only available to those in need under the 1986 Social Security Act (see Ogus et al, 1995 and Fredman, 1997 for further details).

[8] However, in 1988 (under Thatcher's government 1979-90) this fund was dismantled and instead employers were given the responsibility (and costs) for administering payments with the right to reimburse themselves through deductions from their own liability to pay National Insurance.

Appendix 2: BBC occupational groups by female concentration, sex and pay grade

Job no	Occ group	No total staff	% female	Senior managers		Pay grade 10/11		Pay grade 9		Pay grade 8		Pay grade 7		Pay grade 6		Pay grade 5		Pay grade 4		Pay grade 3		Pay grade 2		Pay grade 1	
				M	F	M	F	M	F	M	F	M	F	M	F	M	F	M	F	M	F	M	F	M	F
1	HRJ	50	98														1	1	26		18		1		2
2	SFP	92	98														6	1	36		48	1			
3	SFQ	775	97													1	3	2	61	15	528	9	152		4
4	HRT	210	87	1			3	14	38		3	10	45				21	3	53		17				1
5	RPC	595	86									1	1			38	80	12	56	31	371	1	2		1
6	FFR	42	86					2							1			2	24	2	11				1
7	TPC	823	83									1	3	1	5	118	243	4	417	4	7	3	9	6	2
8	ASQ	50	82																2	7	34	2	4		
9	ASP	730	81							1		3		4	3	11	32	26	95	36	206	49	222	10	31
10	OPJ	62	81														4	1	17	6	10	2	18		1
11	PMU	181	80			2		3	2	2	3	15	52	8	32		6	3	11	3	33	1	4		
12	NJC	576	80									1	3	1	2	38	69	16	64	62	321				
13	ASE	58	79								1			1	4		8	2	11	8	17		4		
14	FMQ	120	78													2	1	3	8	3	11	9	71	9	3

Job no	Occ group	No total staff	% female	Senior managers		Pay grade 10/11		Pay grade 9		Pay grade 8		Pay grade 7		Pay grade 6		Pay grade 5		Pay grade 4		Pay grade 3		Pay grade 2		Pay grade 1	
				M	F	M	F	M	F	M	F	M	F	M	F	M	F	M	F	M	F	M	F	M	F
15	NJT	78	78							1	1	3	9			12	50		—	1	—						
16	TDP	64	78							3	2	2	9				2	1	3	4	17	4	16		1		
17	TPE	47	77	2					1	2	3			1	3	4	4	2	14	2	10		1				
18	PMV	70	76				1		1	1	5	2	3	1	7	3	5	3	13	3	8	4	11				
19	LFJ	79	75											2	11				38	2	7		2				
20	LFP	153	73	2		2	5	11	11	5	8	1	7	15	46		2	6	9	—	20						
21	TPQ	156	72			2		3	4	3	24	15	14		13	10	23	3	9	6	23	1	2				
22	PMF	42	69	2		3	4	—	3	3	3	4	2		7		4		4		2						
23	CSR	48	67		1	3	—	3	9	4		4	4		2			4	9		4		1				
24	FFK	434	67	1		—	4	10	2	4		—	3	2	3	42	40	18	38	34	88	30	102	2	8		
25	FMT	169	66												2		—	9	4	5	30	20	69	23	5		
26	NJF	52	65	6		13	8	2	3	3	13		2		5		2	1			—						
27	TPG	52	63		1	3	5	3	1	1	3	2	2		8	3	7		6								
28	FMS	40	63																6	3	5	8	11				
29	TPR	50	62								1	11	20		1	2	—	5	—					3	8		
30	TPP	194	59									4	5	20	19	39	45	2	7	7	36	7	10				
31	LRS	306	59												2	29	48	96	129	—	—						
32	PMX	62	58	2	1	2										3	2	4	18	10	11	2	2				
33	PMM	68	57	11	9	8	11	6	5	3	14	1		4		3	2					—	2		2		

Job no	Occ group	No total staff	% female	Senior managers M	F	Pay grade 10/11 M	F	Pay grade 9 M	F	Pay grade 8 M	F	Pay grade 7 M	F	Pay grade 6 M	F	Pay grade 5 M	F	Pay grade 4 M	F	Pay grade 3 M	F	Pay grade 2 M	F	Pay grade 1 M	F
34	PMW	144	57	3	1	4	4	9	3	8	10	14	13	3	5	7	15	2	6	8	14	4	7		4
35	HRM	51	57	15	7	1	5	6	16						1										
36	OPE	121	56					9	1	8	3	4	2	6	5	4	13	5	15	15	27	1	2		
37	TPB	1,046	55			37	12	157	154	9	7	208	318	41	54	2	4	2	1	8	18	9	5		
38	LRP	304	54											3						61	80	45	53		
39	EST	112	53			5	3	6	6	29	5	10	7		6	8	11	1	12	2	11				
40	RPB	565	52			4		18	7	75	58	172	223		6		6		1						
41	NJD	52	52				1			10	7	6	9	1		9	10								
42	RPD	60	48						1	4	5	16	12	3	1	4	8	1	1	3	2				
43	TPA	148	48	2		38	34	26	26	2	4	7	6			2			1						
44	FFP	154	47			4	3	16	13	29	26	12	8	11	8	6	9								
45	RPA	47	45		1	9	4	11	11	4	4	2	1												
46	NJR	2,811	44			119	35	147	63	571	399	226	250		1	508	487	1			3				
47	TPM	267	44	25	16	66	46	30	16	24	26	4	8	1			2		2		1				
48	TPD	104	41			3		14	7	2		15	15	1		3	4	23	16		1				
49	RPM	81	41	10	7	16	12	14	11	4	1	4	1												
50	FFM	94	40	19	6	12	8	11	8	13	4	1	9		1				1						
51	FFF	101	39	14	7	12	4	9	9	11	5	4	6	8	4	3							3		
52	NJB	545	38			4	3	5	5	86	42	236	152	5	3	1	1		1						
53	CSM	42	38	16	7	7	8	3	1												1				

Job no	Occ group	No total staff	% female	Senior managers M	Senior managers F	Pay grade 10/11 M	Pay grade 10/11 F	Pay grade 9 M	Pay grade 9 F	Pay grade 8 M	Pay grade 8 F	Pay grade 7 M	Pay grade 7 F	Pay grade 6 M	Pay grade 6 F	Pay grade 5 M	Pay grade 5 F	Pay grade 4 M	Pay grade 4 F	Pay grade 3 M	Pay grade 3 F	Pay grade 2 M	Pay grade 2 F	Pay grade 1 M	Pay grade 1 F
54	TDQ	233	37					4	5	61	42	32	18	12		18	10	17	11	2	1				
55	NJA	561	35	4		116	58	83	44	38	19	84	49	40	24				1						
56	TDU	40	33							14	4	8	9			2						1			
57	ITQ	225	31			2		4	6	18	7	36	13	75	26	11	3	3	3	5	7	1	4		
58	NJM	274	29	46	17	94	34	43	20	10	9														
59	FMM	159	28	6	2	5		9	2	16	3	20	4	37	18	8	4	4	4	2	3	10	2	7	2
60	ITK	110	27									10	1	15	1	33	6	8	6	4	4	10	12		
61	ITF	72	22	4	2	8	2	23	3	6	2	12		3			2		2		1				
62	OPU	794	18						1	68	1	176	10	204	40	186	88	15	5						
63	OPS	558	18							20		385	76	4		38	16	10	7						
64	OPT	110	16					1						25		61	16	2		15	2	2			1
65	BEK	51	16													2			4			14		10	
66	OPM	209	14	4	2	46	2	76	9	27	5	25	11												
67	OPQ	208	14							17		22	2	5	23	47	4	88							
68	OPW	189	13									54	8	55	4	53	10		1			1			
69	AST	45	11													3		3		6		29	2	2	3
70	OPP	326	8							104		33	1	3	2	153	19	6	2	1			1		
71	BEP	168	7							8		46		102	10				1						
72	ITX	57	7	3				8		9		24	2	5		2							1		
73	OPK	270	6													21		38	5	175	8	14		4	2

Job no	Occ group	No total staff	% female	Senior managers		Pay grade 10/11		Pay grade 9		Pay grade 8		Pay grade 7		Pay grade 6		Pay grade 5		Pay grade 4		Pay grade 3		Pay grade 2		Pay grade 1	
				M	F	M	F	M	F	M	F	M	F	M	F	M	F	M	F	M	F	M	F	M	F
74	GEW	131	4			6		51	3	16	1	35		5	1	13									
75	BEQ	590	3					3		23	1	205	7	318	11	10		10	1				1		
76	TDK	97	3													27		52	1	15	2				
77	BER	104	3					23		48	1	24	1	4		2									
78	BEM	94	2	3		14	2	25		34		16													
79	BEL	87	0											5		32		46		2				2	

Source: Data collected by author from BBC Human Resources Department

Note: Occupational groups of less than 40 omitted. Data collected 1998. See overleaf for key to job numbers and occupational groups.

Typical job within an occupational group

#	Code	#	Code	#	Code	#	Code
1	HRJ: personnel assistant	26	NJF: head of language section	51	FFF: management accountant	76	TDK: tele design operative
2	SFP: personal assistant	27	TPG: department management	52	NJB: news producer	77	BER: installation engineer
3	SFQ: secretary	28	FMS: reprographic worker	53	CSM: commissioning management	78	BEM: engineering management
4	HRT: personnel officer	29	TPR: script editor	54	TDQ: graphics	79	BEL: technician
5	RPC: radio production support	30	TPP: floor/stage management	55	NJA: news editorial		
6	FFR: finance assistant	31	LRS: professional librarian	56	TDU: scenic design		
7	TPC: television production support	32	PMX: viewer/listener relations	57	ITQ: IT development/analysis		
8	ASQ: allocations support	33	PMM: press/publicity manager	58	NJM: news manager		
9	ASP: management assistant	34	PMW: sales/marketing	59	FMM: facilities management		
10	OPJ: resources management support	35	HRM: personnel manager	60	ITK: IT user support		
11	PMU: Publicity officer	36	OPE: resources coordinator	61	ITF: IT management		
12	NJC: news research	37	TPB: television producer	62	OPU: sound		
13	ASE: scheduling assistant	38	LRP: library services	63	OPS: picture editing		
14	FMQ: facilities support	39	EST: trainer	64	OPT: post production		
15	NJT: teletext/subtitling	40	RPB: radio producer	65	BEK: broadcasting engineering technical support		
16	TDP: costume	41	NJD: news presentation	66	OPM: operations manager		
17	TPE: tele planning/coordination	42	RPD: radio presentation	67	OPQ: lighting		
18	PMV: press/publicity specialist	43	TPA: television editorial staff	68	OPW: technical operator		
19	LFJ: legal support	44	FFP: business manager	69	AST: storekeeper		
20	LFP: contracts and negotiations	45	RPA: radio editorial staff	70	OPP: camera person		
21	TPQ: programme finance	46	NJR: journalist	71	BEP: communications engineer		
22	PMF: chief publicity officer	47	TPM: television management	72	ITX: IT infrastructure		
23	CSR: channel management	48	TPD: television presentation	73	OPK: rigger driver		
24	FFK: finance support	49	RPM: radio management	74	GEW: engineering specialist		
25	FMT: premises operations	50	FFM: finance management	75	BEQ: maintenance engineer		

Appendix 3: BBC pay grades

Pay grade	London		Outside London	
	Minimum	**Maximum**	**Minimum**	**Maximum**
1	£10,740	£15,540	£8,240	£13,040
2	£11,811	£17,230	£9,311	£14,730
3	£13,088	£19,260	£10,588	£16,760
4	£14,572	£21,600	£12,072	£19,100
5	£16,261	£24,270	£13,761	£21,770
6	£18,197	£27,340	£15,697	£24,840
7	£20,381	£30,790	£17,881	£28,290
8	£22,853	£34,700	£20,353	£32,200
9	£25,572	£39,000	£23,072	£36,500
10	£28,291	£43,300	£25,791	£40,800
11	£31,340	£48,120	£28,840	£45,620
Senior	Not stipulated	Not stipulated	Not stipulated	Not stipulated

Source: BBC Salary Ranges (1998)

Note: For the purposes of simplification, the London salaries were used for all BBC employees under analysis. The senior grades' salaries are not stipulated in the above table but there are four levels. In order of hierarchy, the lowest is senior manager (SM) 2, followed by SM 1, the board of managers (which are all on grade SM 1) and finally the most senior is the executive committee whose salaries ranged from £198,000 to the director general's salary of £387,000. Although the board of managers and the executive board are not included in the general quantitative analysis (as these are jobs with less than 40 people in them) their salaries are used here to give an upper bracket to the senior management salaries. Hence we can take the senior pay band to be from £45,620 (top figure of pay grade 11) to the director general's salary.

Index

Page references for notes are followed by n

Printed and bound by CPI Group (UK) Ltd, Croydon, CR0 4YY

23/04/2025

14661025-0002